PATIENCE

broadview editions
series editor: Martin R. Boyne

PATIENCE

edited and translated by Helen Barr

broadview editions

BROADVIEW PRESS
Peterborough, Ontario, Canada

Founded in 1985, Broadview Press remains a wholly independent publishing house. Broadview's focus is on academic publishing; our titles are accessible to university and college students as well as scholars and general readers. With over 800 titles in print, Broadview has become a leading international publisher in the humanities, with world-wide distribution. Broadview is committed to environmentally responsible publishing and fair business practices.

© 2024 Helen Barr

All rights reserved. No part of this book may be reproduced, kept in an information storage and retrieval system, or transmitted in any form or by any means, electronic or mechanical, including photocopying, recording, or otherwise, except as expressly permitted by the applicable copyright laws or through written permission from the publisher. Use of this work in the training of large language models, generative artificial intelligence, and other machine learning programs without the express written permission of Broadview Press is strictly prohibited.

Library and Archives Canada Cataloguing in Publication

Title: Patience / edited and translated by Helen Barr.
Other titles: Patience (2024) | Container of (work): Patience (Middle English poem) | Container of (expression): Patience (Middle English poem). English. (Barr)
Names: Barr, Helen, 1961- editor, translator.
Series: Broadview editions.
Description: Series statement: Broadview editions | Includes bibliographical references. | Poem in original Middle English and in modern English translation.
Identifiers: Canadiana (print) 20240312627 | Canadiana (ebook) 20240312724 | ISBN 9781554815395 (softcover) | ISBN 9781770489684 (PDF) | ISBN 9781460408926 (EPUB)
Subjects: LCSH: Patience (Middle English poem)—Translations into English. | LCSH: English poetry—Middle English, 1100-1500—History and criticism. | LCGFT: Poetry.
Classification: LCC PR2110 .A31 2024 | DDC 821/.1—dc23

Broadview Editions
The Broadview Editions series is an effort to represent the ever-evolving canon of texts in the disciplines of literary studies, history, philosophy, and political theory. A distinguishing feature of the series is the inclusion of primary source documents contemporaneous with the work.

Advisory editor for this volume: Martin R. Boyne

Broadview Press handles its own distribution in Canada and the United States:
PO Box 1243, Peterborough, Ontario K9J 7H5, Canada
555 Riverwalk Parkway, Tonawanda, NY 14150, USA
Tel: (705) 482-5915
email: customerservice@broadviewpress.com

For all territories outside of Canada and the United States, distribution is handled by Eurospan Group.

Broadview Press acknowledges the financial support of the Government of Canada for our publishing activities.

Canadä

Typesetting and cover: George Kirkpatrick

Broadview Press® is the registered trademark of Broadview Press Inc.

PRINTED IN CANADA

Contents

Acknowledgements • 7
Introduction • 9
A Note on the Text • 43

Patience • 45
Notes on the Text and Translation • 75

Appendix A: Scriptural Sources • 89
1. The Old Testament Book of Jonah • 89
2. Christ's Sermon on the Mount: The Beatitudes (Matthew 5:1–12) • 92
3. Psalm 68:2–10; 16–20 • 92
4. The Prophet Iunus, from the *Qur'an*, Chapter 10 • 93

Appendix B: Analogues • 95
1. *Naufragium Jonae Prophetae* • 95
2. *The Prophet Jonah Lost at Sea* • 99
3. From the Middle English Metrical Paraphrase of the Book of Jonah • 103

Appendix C: Other Contemporary Contexts • 105
1. Wycliffite Sermon for All Saints' Day (Matthew 5:1–12) • 105
2. From Dan Michel, *Ayenbite of Inwit or Remorse of Conscience* • 107
    a. From the Virtue of Prowess: The Fourth Degree, Patience • 107
    b. From the Sin of Sloth • 108
    c. From the Sins of the Tongue • 108
3. The Storm Scene from *The Gest Hystoriale of the Destruction of Troy* • 109
4. The Whale from the Middle English *Physiologus* • 111

Appendix D: Visual Materials • 113
1. The illustrations to *Patience* in BL MS Cotton Nero A.x • 113
2. The whale as island from Gerald of Wales's *Topographia Hibernica* • 114
3. A whale opens its mouth and lets out a sweet scent to lure small fish, in a bestiary • 115

    4. The Annunciation: The Holy Spirit as Dove Flies into Mary's Ear • 116
    5. Doom Painting in the Church of Thomas à Becket • 117

Appendix E: Sketch Maps of the Topography of *Patience* • 119
    1. Old Testament • 120
    2. New Testament • 121
    3. Jonah's Journey • 122

Works Cited and Recommended Reading • 123
Image Credits • 127

Acknowledgements

First, I want to thank all those at Broadview Press. Marjorie Mather for commissioning the work and for keeping warm and supportive faith in a project that was delayed at the eleventh hour by a downward turn of Fortune's Wheel. Martin Boyne for his scrupulous but non-intrusive copy editing and buoyant good cheer throughout the process. Thank you to the anonymous readers for wise words and generous good speed.

I'm delighted that Alice Aherne agreed to edit a Latin source for *Patience—Naufragium Jonae Prophetae*—and created such a witty and learned translation of the poem. *Naufragium Jonae* deserves to see the light of day in its own right, and it is also an important contribution to our understanding of *Patience*. I am deeply indebted to Alice, and I am sure that readers will learn so much from reading her work. Thank you to Guy Westwood for introducing us to each other. Simon Armitage very kindly read the first draft of my translation, and his observation that it "had a cheeky grin on its face" let me know that I was on the right track and heartened me to keep going with a cheeky grin of my own.

I owe massive thanks to Annie Sutherland and Laura Varnam for convincing me to finish this and for their determination to make sure that I did—and to Raphaela Rohrhofer and Ayoush Lazikani for backing them up in spades. Thank you to Maria Nikolova for all your care in working on the Middle English text and for being an ideal and judicious reader of the translation.

Thank you Cathy Swire for your vision and creativity in reading my introduction and translation and for sharing your craft. I have learned so much. To David Barr, thank you for reading all of this and for the uplifting conversations we have had about translation, troubling theology, and the perils of placing archaeological treasures in a school tuck-shop. As ever, Vincent Quinn has been the most wonderful academic muse, intellectual companion, and friend. Alan Rusbridger, with his indefatigable competitiveness for trading wicked limericks, helped me to hone my ear for scansion.

There are many others who have contributed so much to making this book, whether they realize it or not: Clare O'Brien, Nancy Campbell, Jacob Farrelly-Holness, Fergus Barr, Aneela Shah, Jane Redman, Sapphire Shoferpoor, Anouska Lester, Matthew Monaghan, Sophie Ratcliffe, Isaac Louth, Jane Hines, Amanda Holton, Nicholas

Perkins, Carol Harrison, Emily Halton, Paul Strohm, and Frances Sunderland. And the warm, generous folk of Cassington.

I came to know and to love *Patience* though sharing it with generations of students at Lady Margaret Hall, Oxford (some of you appear in the preceding paragraphs). All of you have helped me better to understand and to relish Middle English literature. And you have fuelled my passion for making this extraordinarily profound (but linguistically difficult) poem more friendly-facing. Thank you to all of you. What I've tried to do in this edition is to give something back.

Helen Barr
Cassington

Introduction

The Poem

Patience is the third of the four alliterative poems preserved in British Library MS Cotton Nero A.x (fols. 83r–90r). It follows *Pearl* (fols. 39r–55v) and *Cleanness* (fols. 57r–82r) and is followed in turn by *Sir Gawain and the Green Knight* (fols. 91v–124r). All four poems are extant only in Cotton Nero A.x, and all the titles are editorial. *Patience* acquires its name from the repetition of the word "pacience" in its opening and closing lines. It retells the Old Testament story of Jonah (see Appendix A1). The manuscript contains illustrations to the poems (see Appendix D1). There are two for *Patience*: on fol. 86r, the illustrator shows the sailors throwing Jonah from the ship, his feet still in their hands, while the whale lurks in the sea; on fol. 86v, Jonah is shown preaching to the people of Nineveh. The four poems in the codex are commonly thought to be the work of a single author. He has not been identified, but he was clearly very well read. He knew Latin and was well versed in scripture and theology. He was also familiar with a wide range of secular literature in English and French. The poems are generally dated to c. 1370–90s, and studies in the dialect of the manuscript suggest that they were written in south Cheshire, though Staffordshire and Derbyshire are also contenders. It seems likely that the poet was part of an aristocratic household, either as a priest or in some other capacity.

The shortest of the four poems, *Patience* is often described as a "literary homily." It opens with an exposition of the quality of "pacience" (1–8). The narrator then recounts his hearing the reading from St Matthew's Gospel 5:3–10 at a High Mass for the Feast of All Saints (9–28). Lines 29–56 contain the narrator's commentary on the Beatitudes he has heard. From the eight listed, he chooses two as his guides: the first, blessed are those who are poor in heart (13), and the last, blessed are those who can govern their hearts (27). He vows to live in poverty and patience. Lines 29–46 personify each of the eight Beatitudes as courtly women. Lines 34–35 create a ninth Beatitude: he were blessed if he had one of these women, but even more so if he had them all. From this extra-biblical benediction the narrator creates a domestic vignette; shackled to Dame Poverty and Dame Patience, he has to "put up and shut up." Glossing his own predicament, he draws an analogy between having to obey his lord's commands, even if that means being sent on an errand to Rome (52). The narrator concludes his "homily" with an exemplum (57). The story of Jonah serves as a warning that if you can't abide suffering, then more troubles will ensue.

Jonah's tribulations occupy the rest of the poem. While the Book of Jonah is the Old Testament source, the poet amplifies the narrative with poetic panache and bristling theology. Less a biblical paraphrase and more a dramatic reinterpretation, the poet fleshes out the characterization of Jonah's struggles with God, especially with the recreation of voice. God's first words to Jonah rush boisterously into his ear; he teases him, mocks him, and cuts him down to size (along with the precious plant that Jonah thought his protection). But lest we think God simply a bully, his closing words tell of compassion for his creation with sublime tenderness. Omnipotent though he be, the suffering of innocents fills his heart with sorrow (507). How could he not be moved to mercy by the plight of those who have lost their sanity, infants sinlessly sucking at the breast, mothers unable to tell one hand from the other, and animals speechless, who cause no harm (509–19)? If God were as rash as Jonah, great harm would ensue. Few would survive (520–21).

For his part, Jonah is peevish, panicky, lazy, and short-sighted. Commanded by God to go to Nineveh to urge the people to repent their sins, he sets out his own conditions: his first word is "If" (75). Thrown into a tizz, he invents his own scenario of what will happen. The treacherous Ninevites will have no truck with his message: he'll be imprisoned, tortured; maybe God wants him dead? Unprepared to meet his imagined fate, Jonah decides to slink off to Tarshish, where God cannot see him. He finds a ship ready to sail at Joppa, pays the sailors to take him on board, and thinks he has escaped God's summons. But God creates a storm which so imperils the ship that the sailors believe they must have some stowaway on board. Jonah is snoring in the "safe" depths of the ship until a sailor kicks him awake and frogmarches him onto the deck to draw lots with the others to determine which of them will be cast overboard. Jonah draws the shortest straw.

The sailors cast him overboard, whereupon God commands a whale to swallow him up. Surrounded by the stench of the whale's guts, his path blocked by filth, he prays to the God he wilfully disobeyed for mercy. We never know why God decides to spare Jonah. After Jonah pledges always to do God's bidding, the next word is "Thenne" (337). God orders the whale to vomit up his prophet, and Jonah reaches dry land. Asked once more whether he will now go to Nineveh, Jonah answers, "Yes, Lord" (347). His prophecy that God will destroy Nineveh within forty days produces terror and repentance. The king tears off his rich robe, puts on sackcloth and ashes, and issues a proclamation that all citizens (and animals) must fast and pray to God for mercy. "And" (407) God forgives them.

Jonah is furious. He berates God for breaking his word. Jonah knew all along that his errand was futile: God sent him to preach vengeance, only for God to show mercy. Feeling branded as a liar, Jonah calls on God to end his life. Rebuked by God for his petulant response, concerned more for his reputation than Ninevite repentance, Jonah chitters his way to a field on the eastern side of the city to sulk and to see what will happen to Nineveh. The sun is scorching, so Jonah builds a makeshift shelter from whatever sparse foliage he can find. With his improvised semi-protection in place, Jonah reprises his inactivity on the ship and goes to sleep.

In the meantime, God causes a great woodbine to bloom out of the ground to protect his somnolent prophet. When he wakes, Jonah is delighted by his new accommodation, capers in joy all day, and then goes to sleep again. God summons a second beast, this time a maggot, which chews up the root of the woodbine. God stills the winds and the clouds so that the sun beats down relentlessly. When Jonah awakes he is angry and distraught. "[H]is" (474) woodbine is destroyed; he has nowhere to hide from the burning sun. He weeps with fury and demands God to tell him why he has treated him so harshly. Why couldn't he just let him die? God's reply explains his compassion for his creation and his care for those who repent their sins and obey him. We are left uncertain where God's voice ends in the poem (if it does) and whether the narrator steps in to conclude. Jonah, however, is given no right of reply. Like the cattle in the last verse of the Book of Jonah, he is silent.

We can accuse Jonah of pride, wrath, envy, covetousness, and sloth (lechery we leave to the narrator). All seven are deadly, and, I contend, in Jonah's case all are emotionally reasonable. The spare Old Testament narrative yields a Jonah whom it is comparatively straightforward to gloss as an exemplar of proud and feeble disobedience to God's will; the *Patience*-poet gives us a Jonah who's more like a textual crux. At every point where Jonah faces a challenge, the poetry compromises didacticism. God's commands are harsh; while his motivations remain inscrutable, his speeches crackle with human tonality. Jonah's panic and terror are described vividly; the list of possible tortures were he to go to Nineveh are added to the biblical source. The horror of spending three days and three nights in the stinking belly of a huge and terrifying fish are magnified by the poet's attention to sensory detail. Who has not wrinkled their nose when reading the poetic tour de force of Jonah's trip down the whale's intestines? God's gift and destruction of Jonah's shelter expands two biblical verses into a detailed account of the time it takes God to create the woodbine, the delight that it brings Jonah, and once more, the languishing sensory description of the heat, the cool, the respite—only for a maggot to munch up the root of the parasol plant within the space of two lines. Why such potent poetry, which immerses a reader or audience in the recreation of felt experience, if the purpose of the poem is to create the kind of homiletic exemplar familiar in sermons or in handbooks of pastoral care? Responses to that question are several, and none of them straightforward. In the sections below—sources, theology, social poetics, the natural world, poetics, fourteenth-century religious debates, and geography—I will endeavour to show that *Patience* is as resistant to answers as any of the four poems in Cotton Nero A.x. Not the least of this is the humour of the poem. While Chaucer is more usually associated with "game" and the *Patience*-poet with "earnest," I will argue that the anonymous genius knew very well that the most honest preaching is inseparable from play.

Sources and Analogues

The Bible

Patience is often described as a biblical paraphrase of the Book of Jonah, and it is. But the poem's biblical reach extends far beyond the Old Testament story of Jonah and the whale. Its retelling is nourished by sources and analogues from a wide range of sources, both verbal and visual.

Before we embark on Jonah's story, the poet has already embellished the recital of the Beatitudes from Christ's Sermon on the Mount, Matthew 5:1–12 (see Appendix A2). While lines 13–28 are a close rendering of the Gospel text, there are some significant variations. Line 25 alters Matthew 5:9 with its promise of blessing for those who make peace. Instead, the children of God are those who hold their peace. While this may show influence of the *Glossa Ordinaria* (bibles in the Middle Ages were often accompanied by a huge textual commentary that surrounded the text, comprising glosses from theologians)—"the peaceful are those who quieten all motions of the soul and subdue them to reason" (*Patrologia Latina*, 114:90)—it also tailors the biblical promise to the poem's emphasis on Jonah's truculence in response to God's commands. The eighth Beatitude promises the kingdom of heaven to those that suffer persecution for justice's sake (Matthew 5:10). *Patience* omits "persecution" and "justice." Line 28 promises salvation to those who practise self-control; the narrator adds, "as I said earlier." This might refer to the first Beatitude or to the seventh, both of which instil the need for humility and self-restraint. More significant is the narrator's omission of Christ's gloss on the eighth Beatitude:

> Blessed are ye when they shall revile you, and persecute you, and speak all that is evil against you, untruly, for my sake. Be glad and rejoice, for your reward is very great in heaven. For so they persecuted the prophets that were before you. You are the salt of the earth. (Matthew 5:11–13)

The narrator's self-referential gloss to his earlier words distracts attention from this crucial omission from the Bible. How would Jonah's tribulations be framed had the narrator included the promise of salvation for persecuted prophets? Salt of the earth Jonah is not, though he becomes thoroughly drenched with the salt of the sea.

The last two verses from the Sermon on the Mount are the ninth occurrence of the anaphoric "Blessed are they." As we have seen, the narrator substitutes a sly ninth Beatitude of his own. Line 30, which urges us to follow the virtues of these lovely ladies, is drawn from a passage in *The Romance of the Rose* (lines 7721–38). This controversial French text was begun by Guillaume de Lorris in 1340 and completed by Jean de Meun about forty years later. *Patience* references the lines in which the Lover is taught by his friend how he can win over his Lady by imitating her virtues. The same passage is paraphrased in *Cleanness*, lines 1057–68. The personification of these eight blessings as courtly ladies in *Patience* allows the narrator to smirk at a more secular "blessing": octogamy—or, second best, possession of at least one of these Dames (34). The frame narration of the Sermon on the Mount is like a series of homiletic Russian dolls: the narrator hears a sermon at Mass which contains Christ's Sermon on the Mount of Olives, which contains the narrator's lewd homily on masculine sexual wish-fulfilment quashed by the outcome of shackled domesticity with two insufferable women. Not quite the model of self-containment that Christ preached to his disciples.

It comes as small surprise, then, that the narrator does not fulfil his promise to recount the story of Jonah "as holy wryt telles" (60). God's biblical word is plain: "Now the word of the Lord came to Jonah" (Jonah 1:1). Lines 62–63 render God's voice as a "glam" that resounds in Jonah's ear abrasively. As other instances of "glam" in Cotton Nero A.x attest, this is a rude awakening: "[s]uch a glauerande glam of gedered rachchez / Ros þat þe rocherez rungen aboute" [The cacophonous baying of the assembled hounds rose so high that the mountain rocks resounded] (*Gawain*, 1426-27; cf. *Patience*, 138-39). No wonder that God's summons makes Jonah "vnglad" (63). The poet's addition of "ere" (64) is intriguing. Images of the Annunciation figure God's word as a dove in a gleam of light that enters Mary's ear (see Appendix D4). Old Norse *glam* ("noise") is a near homophone of Old English *glǽm* ("light"), so might God's entrance into *Patience* be a cheeky tweak on Annunciation iconography? God's word spawns the Incarnation, but—as Jonah speculates in a later addition to the biblical source—God sits on a throne so high in majesty that he couldn't care less if Jonah is captured in Nineveh, stripped naked, and torn to pieces on a cross by a rabble of criminals (94-96). Shockingly, in drawing a parallel between his imagined Nineveh torture and Christ's crucifixion, Jonah conjures an image of a God so indifferent to human suffering that he kills his own son. It can be argued that this is Jonah's imagination, not the poet's; but it is the poet who has created the scenario. There is no equivalent to lines 73-96 in the Bible. On hearing God's command, Jonah simply flees into Tarshish (Jonah 1:4).

The poet expands speech and characterization compared to the Book of Jonah. The narrator interjects to provide commentary on his exemplary narrative (117-28; 245-46; 256-62; 296; and possibly 528-31); the sailors' cross-examination of Jonah bristles with new taunting menace (197-204; Jonah 1:6-8); Nineveh's king tears his "ryche" robe off his back, sits wailing in the dust, and issues a "decre" to his people through his "serjauntes" which covers all manner of people and animals and every "prynce," "prest," and "prelate" (377-433; Jonah 3:6-10). He sounds like a medieval king, and the arrogance with which he asserts that God will have mercy if all repent of their sins (400-06) trumps the biblical king's uncertainty (Jonah 3:10) with his assured knowledge of how God will act: "I wot" (399), and "[h]e wyl" (403).

The characters most embellished are God and Jonah. The compassionate concern expressed in God's final speech for the most vulnerable of his Creation amplifies a brief mention in Jonah 4:11. Added also is God's motivation toward forgiveness for those who come and recognize him as "Kyng" and believe his word. *Patience* turns God's second command to Jonah to go to Nineveh (Jonah 3:1-2) into a snide taunt (346); in his rebuke to Jonah's angry lament (rank noise in God's view) for the loss of his woodbine (Jonah 4:9-11), God squabbles over what is "lyttel," reminds Jonah that he could not be bothered to tend his plant even for an hour, and belittles his prophet's suicidal despair with the snarky comment that Jonah would be prepared to die over a plant that was here one minute and was gone the next (490–500). God may be right, but he is downright rude.

Patience expands the characterization of the biblical prophet to produce a Jonah who is wilful, rash, petulant, frustrated, angry, and scared. Put differently, the poem's Jonah responds to God's brusque caprice in recognizably human terms. To be sure, Jonah's logic is naïvely literal-minded when he thinks that God will not be able to find him if he escapes over the sea because God created only the earth. His glee when the ship sets sail is foolishly myopic, but given the terrors he imagines for himself were he to be captured in Nineveh, his relief is entirely comprehensible. And he does come to his senses. Jonah's speech (Jonah 3:9) is expanded into a humble, dignified confession of guilt which acknowledges God's power (205–12). Jonah's single prayer to God from the whale's belly (Jonah 2:2–10) becomes two supplications heavily laden with descriptions of the torments he suffers. The first (282–88) appeals imperatively to God to set aside vengeance and show mercy since he acknowledges his guilt. Line 288, "And preve þe ly3tly a Lorde in londe and in water," is a curious addition; even as he acknowledges God's power, Jonah's closing comment issues a challenge that sounds more like a vow in a medieval courtly romance than a plea of humility. Jonah's longer confession (305–36) starts with a close, but descriptively expanded, paraphrase of Jonah 2:2–10, which is itself drawn from Psalm 68 (see Appendix A3). From line 323, Jonah and his avatar part company. With great emphasis on the balance between justice and mercy, Jonah promises good behaviour when God saves him (333). His conviction that God will be merciful foreshadows that of the king of Nineveh. The poet has added both to his source. And rather as his first "prayer" ended, Jonah concludes his second appeal with a feudal oath 'haf here my trauthe' (336). Jonah thinks of God as a secular lord whose commands he pledges to obey in return for his protection.

Bound by his secular understanding of obligation, Jonah is furious when God changes his mind and spares the Ninevites. While the biblical Jonah is exceedingly troubled and angrily reminds God that he had predicted this outcome, which is why he fled into Tarshish (Jonah 4:1–4), *Patience*'s Jonah gives God both barrels (413–28). He asks him to be the judge of his own behaviour. The poet dilates Jonah's biblical speech to emphasize how he knew all along that God would be merciful (I analyze the diction of lines 417–19 below). And yet God still made him threaten the proud Ninevites, only for Jonah to be made a liar for preaching God's word.

Non-biblical Materials

The appendices contain translations of the written and visual materials which form the cultural environment of *Patience*. The Prophet Jonah Lost at Sea, *Naufragium Jonae Prophetae* (*NJP*) (PL 171, 1675–78), attributed to Marbod of Rennes (c. 1035–1123), is a witty commentary on the Book of Jonah (see Appendix B1). It is translated into English here for the first time by Alice Ahearne (Appendix B2). While we have no proof that the *Patience*-poet knew this work, there are some intriguing correspondences between details that are not in the biblical story. For instance, there is a strong narratorial presence (*NJP* 1–11; 23–40). Marbod frames Jonah's predicament as a warning against attempting to flee from God, and as an assurance that God will be merciful to those who trust in him. As in *Patience*, Marbod mocks Jonah's foolishness in thinking that he can escape the sight of the Lord (27–30); he provides motivation for Jonah's fearfulness (32–38) which, while not identical to Jonah's speculation, is human characterization not found in the Bible. Marbod also names heathen gods: The Thunderer (65) and Neptune (85). *NJP* describes the terrors of the storm and features a sailor who kicks Jonah awake and rebukes him harshly. The repentance of the king and the Ninevites (132–40) is expanded even more fully than in *Patience*. Marbod focuses on the abandonment of luxury and comfort; the king's purple robes, his crown, his finery, are replaced with ashes and goatskin. His feather bed has now become the ground (132). Might these details have informed *Patience*, lines 157–60, when the mariners cast their fine clothes, caskets, and feather beds out of the ship? The king's proclamation is expanded to include shepherds and farmers—not equivalent to *Patience*'s princes, priests, and prelates, but human detail added notwithstanding. Both *Patience* and *NJP* introduce the ban on children suckling at their mother's breasts.

If the *Patience*-poet knew *NJP* directly, the differences between the two works are as striking as the parallels. Marbod does not describe the insides of the whale. Its appearance, even the storm itself, is not attributed to the might of God. God speaks directly only once: to command Jonah to go to Nineveh; Jonah speaks directly only once: his prophecy to the Ninevites. God is remote and dignified; there are no tantrums, no bargaining, and no woodbine over which to squabble. Marbod concludes his commentary with an encomium on the mercy of God.

Both Marbod and the *Patience*-poet comment on God's miraculous intervention to save Jonah from the whale's digestion. But the whale in *Patience* is a wholly different creature from the Latin commentary. In the Bible, "a great fish" simply swallows Jonah. Marbod emphasizes the whale's size and menace, neither of which prevents his spitting Jonah out onto the very shore to which he disobediently refused to travel. In the Old Testament, the whale, or sea-monster, is called a leviathan. Psalms 73:14 and 103:26 recount God's power over this terrifying beast. Isaiah prophesies that God will slay the leviathan (Isaiah 27:1). In Job 40:20, God vehemently reminds Job that in contrast to the God he curses, he has no power to tame the leviathan.

Commentators have interpreted God's power over the whale as an allegory of the Almighty's victory over Satan. Medieval Last Judgement paintings over church chancel arches figured Hell as a whale/Satan gobbling up the bodies of souls that were damned. Typological interpretation (commentaries in which Old Testament stories were seen as pre-figuration of Christ's actions) saw Jonah's three nights and three days in the whale's stomach to represent the three days and nights that Christ spends in Hell. The connection is made explicitly in Matthew 12:40. Having conquered the devil and released the just, Christ returns to life. *The Middle English Metrical Paraphrase of the Old Testament* (see Appendix B3) mentions the three days and three nights but does not explicitly make the typological connection (13885–96). The *Paraphrase* was written around the same time as *Patience*, but the contrast between the two Middle English versions of the biblical tale of Jonah could hardly be starker. The *Paraphrase* is composed in rhyming twelve-line stanzas, and individual lines carry alliteration. There is very little embellishment of the story, and scarcely any characterization beyond the functional. While the poem is a paraphrase rather than a translation, the poet refrains from artistic flourishes. The whale has no descriptive epithets whatsoever, and no poetic investigation of its insides. It simply swallows Jonah without causing any damage to his bones or flesh. It doesn't even vomit him out. "The fish" just leaves Jonah by a bank.

Elsewhere, medieval texts and visual materials expend great imaginative licence on the whale. In the Latin bestiary called the *Physiologus*, the whale is unequivocally associated with the devil. This text was translated into Old and Middle English; a translation of the Middle English version can be found in Appendix C4. Sailors are caught in a terrible storm. The whale floats in the sea, waiting to lure them to their deaths. Deceived into thinking that the whale is an island, and a refuge from the terrible storm, the sailors disembark. They alight on the "island," build a fire and warm themselves, thinking they are safe from the hostile elements. The whale then dives down to the depths and drowns them. There is an illustration of this scenario from a bestiary in Appendix D2, with additions from Gerald of Wales's *Topographia Hibernica* (Salisbury, late twelfth–early thirteenth century). The whale is also known as the devil in disguise who lures lesser fishes into its maw through the sweet breath that issues from its jaws. This image also appears in another bestiary of around the same date (England, second or third quarter of the thirteenth century; see Appendix D3).

In *Patience*, the whale is not a creature of deceit but rather a great fish that God can command to do his work. There is no doubt, however, that the poet knew of the equation between the whale, Satan, and hell. He describes the whale as a "warlowe" (258). The whale's stomach "stank" like the devil; Jonah's sensory knowledge of his unexpected lodgings "savoured" (a pun on taste and sapience) like hell (274–75). It is the focus on stench that makes *Patience* distinctive. There is no whiff of olfaction either in the Bible or in Marbod. In the *Physiologus*, the whale's most potent weapon is his sweet breath that lures humans to their doom. *Patience* turns sweet devilish beguilement sour. The whale's shitty intestines receive a poetic laparoscopy *sans pareil*. Not only does this bring Jonah's predicament uncomfortably close to an audience's nostrils, but as I argue below, the identification of the whale's stomach with ecclesiastical and courtly space produces powerful social commentary. And it compromises the earnestness of the typological equation between Jonah and Christ.

The opening and closing lines of *Patience* frame its narrative as an exemplum. Patience is a quality, depending on how we gloss "poynt" (1 and 531; see notes to both lines), and a penance. Pain and penance are to be embraced, even if they cause us displeasure. Medieval pastoral literature abounds with pithy sentiments on the value of virtues and the veniality of antithetical vices, of which the appendices contain some representative examples. The circularity of *Patience*, a feature it shares with *Pearl* and *Sir Gawain and the Green Knight*, might suggest a summary judgement on why patience must be endured. The Cotton Nero A.x poet, however, puts wholesome sententiae and received wisdom to the test. The difference between the perfunctory moral platitudes of pastoral texts and the experience of *Patience*'s Jonah is, as I will go on to show, as wide as the whale's huge jaws (268).

The Natural World

The poet's descriptions of the natural world are his most striking embellishments of the biblical story: the whale, the storm, and the creation and destruction of the woodbine. I return to the contents of the whale's stomach in the final section of this introduction. One feature that all three descriptions share, however, is the emphasis on God's power. The presentation of the natural world in *Patience* is neither androcentric nor ecocentric; it is resolutely theocentric. From the sparse account of the storm and the woodbine, the poet whips up a poetic maelstrom. Both biblical episodes mention God's power over the wind: "God sent a great wind to the sea" (Jonah 1:4) and "when the sun was risen, the Lord commanded a hot and burning wind: and the sun beat upon the head of Jonah" (4:7). *Patience* personifies the wind as Zephyrus, Euros, and Aquilon. God controls these winds "at wylle" (130), and they obey his bidding immediately (135–36). God commands angrily (132), and the winds respond in kind. *Patience* transports the word of God moving over the waters (Genesis 1:2) from the Creation of the world to destructive fury. The winds wrestle, the fishes are rudely ripped from their rest at the bottom of the ocean, the waves whip so high that for all the efforts of the sailors to protect their ship, human effort is futile. The trimming of tackle and the baling of water are no match for the anger of the sea. With their sail destroyed, the sailors take up oars. The seething water smashes them. All human effort is futile; against the sound and fury of the sea there is nothing they can do (220).

Storm scenes allow poets who work in alliterative metre to showcase their poetic muscle. The vigour of the verse and the stress of alliterative staves enable robust recreation of vivid drama. (The powerful storm scene from *The Destruction of Troy* is translated in Appendix C3.) But the *Patience*-poet is unique in his stress on God's omnipotence. God's imperious commands transform favourable breeze ("blyþe breþe," 107) into wrestling winds; his fierce order to the whale makes Satan spew a sinner with no brook of delay (337–40).

The episode of the woodbine is also greatly expanded from the biblical source. Once again, God is shown in command. All Jonah's improvised building skills are whittled to naught once God sends a "worme" to munch up the root: a mini devil who obeys God just as instantly as his massive avatar earlier in the poem. The poet intensifies the heat of the Bible not only by the length of its description but through its contrast with the cool breeze that protects Jonah from the sun. Wind once again is to the fore. God can keep his prophet cool so that not even a mote of sun can touch him; and he can force the winds to keep the clouds away from the sun so that all that grows is scorched.

The natural world does not keep the time that humans expect. Just as plain sailing inexplicably (to human perception) becomes a tempest, so too a balmy day can turn overnight into a scorcher. The woodbine episode emphasizes God's control over time, and over cause and event. Overnight, while Jonah sleeps, God creates a beautiful green plant, so large and so leafy that to Jonah it is like a house (450). Overnight, while Jonah sleeps, God sets a maggot to work so that by the time Jonah wakes, his woodbine has been destroyed. Before he even knows it, the sun has crackled the green leaves, crushed them dry with its heat. Neither human time nor phases of change in the natural world constrain God's work. He can make plants grow to full size in the night; he can make the sun's rays fierce at dawn. He can make nature flourish and chop it down to size in an instant: "wap" (499). In thirteen lines (443–55), God grows the woodbine from nought; in one line a maggot chews up its root (467). God's rebuke to Jonah that he did not tend his plant is biblical, but the *Patience*-poet adds in a timescale: "þe tyme of an howre" (498). There is no metrical need for this addition; as in *Pearl*, the human clock of time cannot measure up to God's reckoning. Whenever he pleases, God can grow a shade through grace (443–44) or ravage a root without reason (467). Explanation is absent: God simply does both *while* (443; 467) Jonah sleeps.

Poetics

Like God, the *Patience*-poet challenges narrative expectations. His play with causality creates a story that is explained—and yet remains inexplicable. The poet speeds up time, slows it down, and leaves narrative gaps. The syntax of the long poetic interpolations is out of sync with direct speech and extradiegetic narration; in other words, anything narrated from outside the world of the story. Alliterative metre is supremely suited to what has been called "catalogue," that is, the accumulation of additive detail carried by the alliterative staves of the verse. Alliterative synonyms amplify the focus on detail that produces sequences of events in which time and causality become disconnected.

Jonah's journey to Tarshish shifts the narrative into the present tense: "passes"; "[f]yndes"; "[m]aches" (97–99). The sailors' preparations focus on present-tense busyness: "ruchen"; "[c]achen"; "we3en"; "[g]ederen"; "wynnes" (101–06). The lines pulse with nautical tackle: main-sail, ropes, windlass, anchor weights, bow-line, bowsprit, harnesses, and oars (102–06). Yet when the storm arises, all these safety measures are futile. The sea-tackle bursts, the tiller and the rudder become indistinguishable, the ropes unravel, the mast splinters, and the sail sinks into the sea. The sailors cut all the cords they so carefully fastened and cast them overboard, along with a non-biblical list of luxury possessions: feather beds, fancy clothes, caskets, coffers, and boxes (148–60). All these details dilate the narrative—with immediate effect.

The storm resounds with stressed synonyms: sea, waters, water, waves, abyss, storm-clouds, and streams. Blow and breath are repeated. There is noise: crashing, surging, heaving, and wrestling. Synonyms for dark, anger, and rough abound. And to take us even closer to the eye of the storm, there is the snapshot of the fishes stirred up from their rest. Each extended description immerses us myopically in multiplied detail: each twist and turn of the whale's intestines; the sailors hanging on to Jonah's feet while the great fish gobbles him without any touch of his teeth; hair shirts that bite the Ninevites' bare backs; the hay, ferns, and plants of Jonah's gazebo; the cool dimensions of the green-leaved woodbine under which Jonah capers, lounges, and laughs. The poet steeps us in experiences that tumble forth without connection. That is, their syntax is overwhelmingly paratactic: each action and thing, and what they're like, just happen—simply next.

As I have argued above, the same is true of God's summary actions in the poem: his commands and his decisions. But it is not true of the extended speeches. Whether it be the narrator, Jonah, God, the sailors, or the Ninevite king, direct speech is characterized by argument and causality, both actual and hypothetical. It begins with the narrator's gloss on the Beatitudes. Because he is stuck with Dames Patience and Poverty, he's got to put up with them. If his lord sends him on an errand, there is no point in grumbling since he'll have to go anyway. The narrator's interpolations gloss the action. He chides Jonah for his foolishness in thinking that God will be unable to spy him on the sea, noting that Jonah shoots "shamefully short" because "Omniscient God" has tricks up his sleeve (112–28). The narrator comments on the miracle that Jonah remains undigested in the whale's guts through God's mighty power (256–63). As I discuss in more detail below, the poem concludes with the repetition of "Forþy" (528; 530).

The speeches of the sailors, Jonah, and the king knit cause and effect. Faced with a storm that becomes ever more ferocious, the wisest of the sailors speaks with despair. He fathoms that the reason for the storm is punishment for a stowaway who has angered his god. The sins of the lawless wretch threaten a sinking for them all, so he proposes they draw lots to smoke out the guilty one. Once he is found and thrown overboard, the ruler of the sea will have pity on the rest. Although the sailors are pagan, their spokesman's prediction comes true (169–76). Faced with the prophecy that the whole city of Nineveh will be swallowed up by the earth, the Ninevite king urges his people to penance and privation. If we leave the pleasure of our wicked sins, and step in the paths that God has ordained, he will forsake his wrath and forgive them their sins. The people perform all the penances that the king ordains (397–403), and God, through his goodness, forgives them their sins. Even though he promised otherwise, he withholds his vengeance (407–08). No explicit connection is made between the king's conditional reasoning and God's change of heart.

Jonah, of course, is infuriated that God has not destroyed the city and its people as he said he would (409–28). Confronted by the sailors when he draws the shortest draw, Jonah humbly confesses that he has angered God, and he has been found guilty. He accepts his fate and asks the sailors to throw him out of the ship because otherwise they are doomed. His reasoning is sound, and his logic is proved correct—just not as Jonah could have predicted. His punishment is to be swallowed for his pride. By the laws of nature, the whale ought to have digested Jonah into a stinky bolus. Twice, Jonah calls from the belly of the whale; twice he pleads for mercy because he acknowledges his sins and God's almighty power. In his second appeal, he tells God that if he puts his justice aside, he will rescue his prophet. Jonah pledges to offer sacrifice and bestow a gift on God in return for his life; his logic depends on God rewarding human penitence and obedience with mercy. One should follow the other. We are not made privy to God's thoughts on Jonah's "deal." The next word is "[t]henne": God commands the whale to spit out his prophet.

Thus chastened, Jonah hurries to Nineveh to prophesy destruction. His words are proved wrong, and Jonah is incensed by the damage to his reputation. He tells God he knew all along that he would be merciful. If the Ninevites were penitent, God would save them. That's why he fled to Tarshish because he knew how his task would end. That is not what he said earlier, of course, when he explained his terror in anticipation of the torture feared at the hands of the Ninevites. Jonah's reasoning is based on a faulty human logic that predicts outcomes that are not within human power to control. We see the same pattern of argument in the quarrel over the worth of the woodbine. The architecture of the poem pits experiential verbal richness against the human ignorance of God's control of grammar in eternal time. God's final speech commands causality beyond human comprehension. The double subjunctive "Wer ... were" (520) slides into a conditional, "Couþe I not þole bot as þou, þer þryued ful fewe" [Could I thole only like you do, there'd be few left alive] (521). "[F]ewe" is non-committal. Who they will be, only time will tell, and not by mortal mode of reckoning—but God's.

Theology

The dissonance between human sense perception and grammatical tense articulates a deeply unsettled theology in *Patience*. Our expectations of narrative cause and effect are frustrated. The grammatical syntax of the poem jumps alarmingly between past, present, future, and future conditional. But the conditions of that future are left unspecified. The poem begins and ends in the present tense, and with the declarative sentences that form the backbone to the first episode of the poem: the narrator's account of the Gospel reading for All Saints' Day.

The list of the Beatitudes from Matthew 5:3–10 (lines 11–29) sets out how human beings will be saved. The Beatitudes are the most crucial piece of knowledge that anyone might wish to know; they are what secures eternal life. They tell us what *will* happen if we follow certain behaviours. If we are meek, suffer grief, pursue righteousness, and hold our peace and so forth, then we will see God and the Kingdom of Heaven shall be ours to enjoy. The narrator terms these outcomes a "mede" [reward] (11) that God has promised. The word *mede* suggests a payment in accord with the service that has been performed, "[a]warded to each in accord with what they'd earned" (12). "Hyght" reappears as "behyght" in line 29. The reward of eternal life is granted to us if we love the virtues of the moral qualities of Dame Patience and her fellow women (30–32). Our future bliss is conditional on what we do. The thumping anaphora of the passage gives us a formula that can be followed.

However, it's not so straightforward. The poet has set up an opening salvo in a theological debate. To state that humans can earn salvation if they follow God's edicts on proper behaviour suggests that they have some agency in their ultimate destiny. God sets out the terms of a contract, and if humans fulfil those terms then he will save them. From a human perspective, the contract appears fair and logical, but it's a theological proposition that bristles with difficulties. We might compare the moment in *Piers Plowman* when a priest is sent what appears to be a pardon from God/Truth. It contains the words "*Et qui bona egerunt ibunt in vitam eternam. Qui vero mala, in ignem eternum*" [And those who do well will pass into eternal life. Those who commit evil will go to the eternal bonfire] (B.7.110). To the long-lasting confusion of the narrator—and the poet; he revised the episode in a later version of the poem—and of subsequent readers and critics, the priest tears the pardon in two. In *Patience*, the narrator also supplies us with a kind of "pardon"—a "get out of Hell free card" based on the eight Beatitudes—but then proceeds, rather like the priest in *Piers*, to rip up this neat narrative solution to saving one's soul. The drama of the story of Jonah that follows serves as a poetic gloss to the Gospel. And it is not comfortable reading.

The story is densely populated by characters and creatures who operate on the assumption that work well done brings reward. The narrator frames his service to his Lord as one of "mede" and "hyure" [hire] (55–56). When Jonah agrees terms with the sailors to ship him to Tarshish, he settles with them ("maches") and gives them payment (99) to secure his passage. A bargain has been struck. When the winds of the storm perform God's bidding, they "wyrk" (136). The king of Nineveh describes the predicament of the city as a *quid pro quo*. If the people perform the penance that God demands, then he will have mercy (396). The sailors provide a reverse scenario: they tell Jonah that his punishment is fixed for his evil deeds (203). This economic equation determines Jonah's responses to God. When he calls for mercy from the bowels of the whale, he attempts to secure a contract with God. He offers him a wholesome gift in return for his safety and assures God he will keep his word (335–36). Jonah's mistake is to consider God as a bargaining partner—to apply the laws of fair trade to God's rule of the universe.

But God is not Jonah's equal; their power is not commensurate. God's operations cannot be subjected to the terms of human hire and reward. God's inscrutable omnipotence challenges the fair belief that good works will earn salvation. How do you square that theological circle? The *Patience* poet dramatizes an issue that racked the minds of learned theologians. In God's atonement for human sin through the crucifixion, God could be seen to have entered into a kind of covenant with human beings that held out the promise of salvation. But how could human beings, however virtuous their deeds, be sure of that salvation, without that knowledge supremely compromising God's absolute power and will? The Beatitudes promise just reward that is rational and proportional to deeds performed. But God's actions in the poem show that divine response to the behaviour of his creation is suprarational. God's capacity for mercy and punishment is beyond human comprehension. God created the world; the world cannot hold its Creator to account.

As preceding sections of this introduction have shown, the poet intensifies God's absolute power through expanding and embellishing the biblical story of Jonah. God's rough voice and the register in which he reprimands his prophet or calls on the whale or the winds to do his bidding are harsh and uncompromising. The narrative perspective contrasts God's majestic vision to human short-sightedness. Lines 129–30 are deeply unsettling. While God is inscrutable, his powers of surveillance are absolute: God never sleeps; he is always able to see what his creation is up to, and he has endless resources to intervene as he pleases. That is not an option for his creation. With their ship battered by the storm, the sailors have nothing in their hands to help them; hard work and sage advice are useless. Despite all the toil, their efforts are futile (220–23). God can turn the world upside down so that fish accustomed to rest safely at the bottom of the sea are bounced to the top (143–44). And as we have seen in the discussion of the natural world, God can turn plain-sailing into a terrifying storm without notice, grow and destroy a plant overnight.

God's endless power for destruction, however, is perhaps less frightening than his capricious capacity for mercy. He can overturn the laws of nature in order to save Jonah in the whale (257). He can spare the Ninevites although he had promised otherwise (407–08). The word for "promised," translated here as "decreed," is "bihy3t" (408), the very word used in line 29, translated as "assured," to describe the promises of eternal reward for good behaviour catalogued in the Beatitudes. Jonah tells the sailors that God created the world with a single word (208), but he also goes back on his word, which is what drives Jonah furious. And Jonah has a point. Having risked his life to tell the Ninevites that they will be reduced to pulp, God changes the outcome, which leaves Jonah feeling a liar, his reputation in tatters. If that seems peevish, we might consider God's reasons for sparing the sinners: "I can't be held merciful yet act with malice" (522). "[H]eld" is a literal translation of the Middle English "halden." There is no equivalent to this statement in the biblical tale of Jonah. Isn't this just God's version of Jonah's concern with his reputation, how he is seen?

The parallel between Jonah and God might be overlooked, coming as it does after God's moving account of why he has saved the Ninevites. The poet distends God's speech in Jonah 2:10–11. God tells Jonah that having laboured for such a long time to create human beings, should he destroy Nineveh, the pain of losing such a place would sink into his heart (507). Many there still weep for their sins, among them those with reduced mental capabilities (509–11), innocent children who have never caused any trouble (513), women "too overwrought" to tell left from right (514–15), and "dumb beasts" incapable of sin or penance (516–17). The poet's repointing of his source emphasizes God's sorrowful reluctance to destroy the innocent. In a striking addition, God upbraids Jonah: "Were I as rash as you are, all would be wrecked / Could I thole only like you do, there'd be few left alive" (520–21). Line 521 reprises the narrator's advice in line 7. For all his dramatization of God's omnipotence, inscrutable to human rationality, the close of the poem tells of God's own suffering. The poem's injunction to practise patience begs a profound question: Who suffers more—God, or the human beings he created?

That question generates further conundrums. If God is so powerful, why does he create such suffering in the first place? His trial of Jonah is explicable on account of the prophet's recalcitrance and his sins of pride and sloth. We could argue that the Ninevites deserve to suffer and to perform penance because they have forsaken God's teaching. We could extend that argument to the suffering of the sailors in the storm: they are pagan. But how does that account for the suffering of the innocents in Nineveh? The babies at the breast whom the king commands should not be fed; the cattle who are forbidden to graze; or those whom God created who lack the capacity to tell right from wrong or one hand from the other? We could argue that their suffering is unnecessary; they are collateral damage. As are the sailors: a breath (which must be God's) puffs them to dry land, but their ship and the cargo they carried are destroyed. (I return to this issue in the section on social poetics below.) God repeatedly terms his Creation his "hondewerk" (496; see also 131, 257); it is what he has made with his own hands. He might be justified in destroying the woodbine he makes for Jonah because Jonah never bothered to look after it; he just took it for granted. But it is hard to make the same argument about the sailors and their ship. We assume the whale is big and ugly enough to endure a spot of indigestion, but what about the innocent fish? And why, if God's heart is so pierced by the suffering of the blameless, does he create humans without full mental capacity?

The Institutional Church

How does this unsettled theology resonate with the debates that were happening when the poem was written? There is nothing in the poem that explicitly questions basic tenets of Christian doctrine. That said, the poem sails rather close to the wind. I have noted above that Jonah's reasons for trying to get out of going to Nineveh are added to the biblical source:

"Our Lord lounges aloof on his lofty perch,
Glowing in glory, and wouldn't give a damn
Were I nabbed in Nineveh and stripped naked
On a cross, sharked shamefully by a crew of scum." (93–96)

The image of Jonah stripped naked and torn apart "[o]n rode" (96) by vagabonds unmistakably suggests Christ's crucifixion. Shockingly, the poet has Jonah imagine God, sitting in glory, far out of reach, complacently indifferent to the slaughter of his own son, which he himself commanded. The typological connection between Jonah and Christ, which in the biblical text offers the comfort of deliverance after three days of torment, is transformed into a speech that destroys the doctrinal teaching on the Holy Trinity. Did one member of the Trinity kill another? While the speech is in Jonah's mouth, and Jonah is wrong, the poem nevertheless voices a heretical inversion of the typological connection between Jonah's three nights in the whale's belly and Christ's three days between his death and resurrection.

Those lines were written at a time when the power of the institutional Church in England was under attack. The ideas of the Oxford philosopher John Wyclif (c. 1320–84) were taken up by supporters from across the social spectrum: from nobility to artisans. One of the key tenets of Wycliffism—or Lollardy—was that the Bible should be translated into English and be made available to all. The official text of the Bible was in Latin, situating it firmly within the institutional hands of the male clerical elite. Preachers, of course, would cite their pericope text (the words of the biblical text they had selected to form the basis of their sermon) in English and continue to expound its significance in the vernacular, but until followers of Wyclif translated the Bible into English in the 1380s and 1390s, a lay readership had no access to this privileged text, unless it were read for them. *Piers Plowman* envisages a cleric doing this for Mede (a secular aristocratic woman) in an early part of that poem (B.3.347). Biblical translation was not formally condemned as heretical until the publication of the act named *De haeretico comburendo* (Of the burning of heretics) in 1401. Even before that date, however, the association of biblical translation with Wycliffism was certainly part of common cultural currency.

As we have seen, *Patience* makes the Book of Jonah available to the laity in English. There is also translation of the Gospel text from Matthew. In both cases, the significant embellishments of the biblical text raise awkward theological questions for the audience or readership—in English. I am not crudely trying to suggest that the author of *Patience* was a follower of Wyclif's teachings: challenges to church authority ranged from orthodox criticism of corrupt practices to radical dissent, to calls for the whole fabric and power structures of the institutional Church to be demolished. To situate any literary text written in the latter part of the fourteenth and early fifteenth centuries along that continuum is no easy task; the picture is too blurred, and much of the evidence is missing. We do not know, for instance, who wrote *Patience*, where it was written, or for whom. Were anyone to read the poem who sympathized with the challenge to the monopoly of the Church on theological debate and religious practices, however, they would find plenty of food for thought.

Indeed, none of the poems in Cotton Nero A.x depict a favourable view of ecclesiastical space. Jonah enters the whale's belly like "a dust-speck sailing through the door of a church" (268). The simile equates the stinking belly of the whale (hell) with a church building. Put starkly, the material church is not only full of excrement but also the gateway to damnation. Whether or not this was the poet's intended meaning, it is entirely possible to read that line to chime with the Wycliffite view that the Church on earth belonged to Antichrist, and the only true church was in Heaven (see Appendix C1). And it is from the putrid church on earth that Jonah calls out to God to save him. He asks for his prayer for mercy to enter God's holy house: "ut veniat ad te oratio mea, ad templum sanctum tuum" [that my prayer may come to thee, unto thy holy temple] (Jonah 2:9; cf. line 328). He pleads that although he is abject, cast out from the sight of the Lord, he surely hopes to walk in his temple and to be at one with him: "Abjectus sum a conspectu oculorum tuorum; verumtamen rursus videbo templum sanctum tuum" [I am cast away out of the sight of thy eyes: but yet I shall see thy holy temple again] (Jonah 2:5; cf. lines 314–16). Comparison with the Vulgate shows that the poet follows the biblical text closely here. But there are crucial shifts; whether because of alliterative exigency or for some more profound reason, it is hard to determine conclusively. The Latin uses the word for "temple" in both instances. The Middle English "holy hous" (328) chimes with the often-used description of the medieval material church as the House of God on Earth derived from Genesis 28:17. So Jonah calls from a fetid church building for his prayer to enter God's Church. Lines 314–16 substitute the verb "trede" for the biblical "look" ("conspectu oculorum") and add the phrase "teme to þyseluen" [be at one with you; literally "belong to you"]. While Jonah and his biblical avatar are both arrogant in their assumption that they will yet see God, it is the juxtaposition of the church that is the whale's belly with God's church in heaven that is problematic.

A key tenet of the most extreme Wycliffite propositions was that the material church on earth was useless. The only true church was the Congregation of the Elect in Heaven. Unless the need for alliteration constrained the poet's word choice (with which I sympathize), the poem has travelled some distance from the promises of the Beatitudes.

If the material church on earth belongs to Antichrist rather than to God, then there is no place for priests to administer sacraments. In *Patience*, the relevant sacrament is confession. It was divided into three parts: oral confession, contrition, and penance. Orthodox theology ruled that oral confession must be made to a parish priest. There are three confessions in *Patience*: by Jonah (twice) and by the Ninevites. In each case, the contrite penitents speak directly to God. Of course, they must; it is the Old Testament after all. The New Testament church on earth has not been invented yet. That said, the poet precedes the account of Jonah with the vignette of the narrator listening to the Gospel reading at a High Mass on All Saints' Day. Strikingly, there is no description of the church building and no mention of priests, nor of how the narrator hears the words of Matthew. Liturgical time and a Eucharistic service are invoked, only for such trappings to be abandoned once we enter the Jonah narrative, apart from the reference to the church door. Radical Wycliffite thought maintained that oral confession to a parish priest was unnecessary, for only God had the power to forgive sin. A prayer in a field was as good as a prayer in a church.

In *Patience*, God has supreme power over the forgiveness of sins. There is no intermediary, unless, of course, we think of the narrator as an intermediary between the biblical text and his interpretation of its meaning—that gets us into even choppier waters. The narrator's lewd gloss on the Beatitudes would surely have earned a clerical frown. And then the narrator concludes the poem with a chippy platitude delivered in the present tense which leaves no room for a member of the institutional Church to help anyone who endures suffering. There's no injunction, for instance, to go to your parish priest for confession, even though the Lateran Council of 1215 decreed that a parishioner must attend confession with their parish priest at least once a year. We could, of course, turn all of this argument on its head. What if the poem is depicting precisely what can happen in the absence of any firm, orthodox, institutional guidance? With no firm hand on the tiller, no sacraments, no pastoral instruction, human beings are as lost, bewildered, and truculent as Jonah. That is, they are in greater danger of damnation, denied, as they are, proper pastoral support to keep them on the straight and narrow. Every time I read *Patience* my views on its ecclesiology and theology shift like so many grains of sand.

Social Poetics

The religious debates in *Patience* are inseparable from commentary on the poet's contemporary social environment. The relationship between God and Jonah is also a relationship between an aristocratic lord and his worker. That is, their interpersonal dynamic reproduces a feudal association. The land belongs to God in perpetuity; he made it. The people belong to him as long as they obey his words. God is like a king or powerful nobleman, and Jonah is one of his retainers. As we have seen, an addition to the biblical source is the word "teme" (316); Jonah belongs to God. As early as line 10, the poem uses the word "meyny"—a band of retained servants—to describe Jesus' disciples. The same word is used in *Pearl* (960 and 1127) to describe those who are blessed in the Kingdom of Heaven. The narrator in *Patience* figures himself as a servant to a lord (51–56), hired to do his bidding. There is no point in chittering his displeasure if asked to perform a task that he does not like, because his lord is more powerful than him and he'll end up in a worse plight.

Viewed in terms of aristocratic feudalism, God may be seen as a tyrannical lord with little feeling for his subjects. Jonah expresses this view when he complains that God lounges loftily in the lap of soft cloud and couldn't care less if his servant is put to death (92–96). God is like a distant ruler, so far above his subjects in his time for leisure that he has no feelings for those he commands. The poem shows that Jonah is misguided in this assumption: God might be in heaven, but his immanent power is always present in the world. He works constantly to protect his handiwork; he never sleeps, nor does his power, even if Jonah thinks the opposite is true (86; 109–17; 323). The only person in the narrative who finds it hard to stay awake is Jonah himself. And God's final speech makes it abundantly clear that he feels for the suffering of his subjects even if they have disobeyed him.

Aristocratic power poses problems in other sections of the poem, however. The king of Nineveh is quick to act when the news of the people reaches him: the city is about to be destroyed. Faced with imminent destruction, he orders a decree to be proclaimed (385–96). He summons his "serjauntes" [officers] (385) to drive out the edict that he has framed at his own judgement (386). It could be argued that in such an emergency, a delay to seek counsel would be inappropriate, and it is the voice of the people and their actions that cause the king to respond. But the diction of line 385 invokes a legal or bureaucratic structure that the king's immediate and individual judgement bypasses. The emphasis on autocratic power and the suffering of the innocents are both amplified from the biblical source: "Et clamavit, et dixit in Ninive ex ore regis et principum ejus, dicens : Homines, et jumenta, et boves, et pecora non gustent quidquam : nec pascantur, et aquam non bibant. Et operiantur saccis homines et jumenta, et clament ad Dominum in fortitudine : et convertatur vir a via sua mala, et ab iniquitate quae est in manibus eorum" [And he caused it to be proclaimed and published in Nineveh from the mouth of the king and of his princes, saying: Let neither men nor beasts, oxen nor sheep, taste any thing: let them not feed, nor drink water. And let men and beasts be covered with sackcloth, and cry to the Lord with all their strength, and let them turn, everyone, from his evil way, and from the iniquity that is in their hands] (Jonah 3:8–9).

The re-pointing of his cruel injunction may have been influenced by lines in Marbod's *Naufragium*. Lines 136–45 amplify the episode to include "council of great men," "the courtier and the soldier," and "a herald." Both the cruelty toward women and babies with the ban on suckling, and the order that farmers cease to feed their beasts, also have a direct parallel in *Naufragium*. Read through a social perspective, which the diction of *Patience* invites, the king of Nineveh issues an absolutist edict that punishes those incapable of sin. It is entirely possible to read the Ninevite section as a commentary on the abuse of earthly feudal power. It makes for uncomfortable reading, given that God is figured as an aristocratic lord. If the poet was influenced by *Naufragium*, however, it is important to note that the Latin poem ends with this episode of the story of Jonah. *Patience* continues, and God speaks with great tenderness and compassion for the most powerless members of society.

We have seen in the section on sources that *Naufragium*'s dramatization of the Ninevite king's repentance emphasizes the renunciation of aristocratic luxury. The king discards his marks of pride: his disdain to come down from his distinguished throne; his crown and his purple robes. His feather bed is now the hard ground, sad sighs replace the music of the lyre, bright colours are replaced by the gloom of wretchedness (121–33). There is no mention of the crown in *Patience*, but the king does abandon his throne, tear the rich robe from his back, and lie in the dust (378–83). None of these details appear in the biblical source. While the poet does not go to the extremes of Marbod, when penitence is at its most urgent, the trappings of aristocracy are the first to go—to be replaced by ash and bare-backed prostration on the ground.

Marbod's feather beds make no appearance in this section of *Patience*, but beds and bedrooms appear at other points in the poem. Jonah enters the whale through the door of a church and stumbles into what seems to be a fine hall (272). Ecclesiastical space morphs into an aristocratic dining area. The collision between sacred and secular points toward the appropriation of the church by the nobility and, in turn, the worldly luxury enjoyed by contemporary clergy. The narrator's gloss on the architectural interiors of the whale's stomach provides an extra twist: "Some bedroom for the bloke who'd bailed out!" (276). "[B]our," derived from French, is not just any old place of slumber; it is a lavishly aristocratic resting space—except, in this instance, the bedroom is a smelly tangle of intestinal filth. Church space is not only inseparable from noble space, but both are collapsed into a place of sleep. The only other instance of "bour" in *Patience* describes the makeshift shelter that Jonah builds on the outskirts of Nineveh (437). Translated there as "boudoir," Jonah's booth, made from whatever foliage he can forage from his barren surroundings, is a place where he goes to sleep (as he also does, of course, in the whale). If Jonah's slumbers in his "bedrooms" can be interpreted as an instance of sloth or despair, which along with pride are the two most deadly of all the Deadly Sins, what does that say about the poet's association of the fetid whale's bedroom with the Church and with the ruling elite?

Marbod's catalogue of the king's renunciation of aristocratic finery includes the substitution of a feathered bed for the dust of the ground. There are no feather beds in this section of *Patience*, but they do appear in the list of goods that the mariners throw from the ship in the attempt to lighten the boat to save their lives. Discarded with the beds are "fashionable clothes, / Caskets, coffers, and precious crafted boxes" (158–59). These are all "bale" (157). I read this diction as a pun: *bale* can be ballast or cargo (*MED* bāle n. (3)), and also woe, torment, or danger (*MED* bāle n. (1) 2a). My translation, "burden," attempts to capture both senses. Finery is a package that is freighted with risk. Lines 158–59 have been added to the biblical source. They are more nuanced than the Ninevite king's renunciation of aristocratic trappings. The fine items would not have belonged to the mariners; they would be the cargo that the noble rich or merchants had paid them to ship from Joppa. The poet of the *Metrical Paraphrase*, in a rare expansion from the biblical source, makes this point clear (see Appendix B3). In *Patience*, the result of God's intervention with the unexpected storm results in loss for those nameless nobles, but crucially, loss for the anonymous mariners as well. They have been hired to perform a service that they do not complete. Furthermore, the long technical list of the mariners' tackle (101–06) demonstrates that these are skilled workers. Despite all of their hard work to set the ship to sail, and to save it from wreckage, their attempts are futile. The mariners' lives are saved, but what of their livelihoods? *Patience* contains an intriguing social vision: the Church and the nobility are associated with sin and hell, and those who are the most vulnerable—women, children, the mentally ill, and animals—are the subject of God's compassion. Skilled artisans who provide services for the rich are left stranded somewhere, the tools of their trade floating like so many pieces of flotsam and jetsam on an unnamed sea. Their commission is sunk to the bottom of the ocean. The poem asks searching questions about the workings of theological reward—and about the inequitable treatment of those whose working lives depend on the payment of those who employ them.

Geography

The action of the poem takes place in various locations in what is now loosely termed "the Middle East." Nineveh is in Mosul, Northern Iraq; Joppa is a port in the southern and oldest part of Tel Aviv in Israel. Tarshish is either the historic city of Tarsus in south-central Turkey, just inland from the Mediterranean, or the ancient city of Tartus on the Mediterranean coast of Syria. All of these locations are biblical. Mapping them enables us to see that when Jonah is commanded to preach in Nineveh, he attempts to flee in the opposite direction. The poet also introduces places that are not in the book of Jonah: Rome, Judea, Israel, Ephraim, the Hermon Hills, and Samaria. The geography of the poem creates a map of holy lands which never existed all at the same time. Old Testament geography merges with New Testament time. In turn, this impossible cartography is prefaced by fourteenth-century time and place in the narrator's introduction to the story. As the maps in Appendix E show, the difficulty of charting the territory of the poem continues to the present time of writing.

Rome is introduced into the story of Jonah by the narrator (52). It is a destination to which he does not wish to go despite his superior's bidding. And it is an intriguing addition, since Rome is the seat of the papacy. When *Patience* was written, there had been a papal schism (in 1377), and there was also a pope in Avignon, France. The schism was a source of controversy and conflict. Well before Henry VIII (r. 1509–47) severed ties with Rome and became the head of the Church of England, Rome was a byword for corruption and insatiable desire for power. Wycliffites regularly termed the pope the

Antichrist. Orthodox criticism bewailed the power of the papacy to issue pardons and indulgences as remission from sin, which prevented proper contrition and left human beings vulnerable to damnation. "Rome" in *Patience* may be an alliterative expedience, though "Rome-runners" is used in an anti-clerical passage in *Piers Plowman* (B.4.127), and the practice of sending clerics on errands to Rome was an established complaint.

References to places in the Middle East create further intriguing issues. Twice, in an addition to the biblical book, *Patience* locates Jonah's home in Judea (57 and 61), and it also adds the detail that Jonah was God's prophet to the Gentiles (62). When the mariners interrogate Jonah—where is he from, what is his mission?—the biblical Jonah says he is a Hebrew. *Patience* adds "of Israyl borne" (205). Israel did exist as a territory in the Old Testament and was separate from Judea, but in the New Testament Israel disappears from the map. The poem highlights Jonah's Jewishness (109; 182; 245) and adds to the biblical details of Jonah's "kyth" [home(land)] (462), "High up on Ephraim or the Hermon Hills" (463). Ephraim, named for the leader of one of the twelve tribes of Israel, was a separate territory from Judea. The Hermon Hills are in the north on the border between Israel and Aram (Syria). So where exactly is Jonah's home? On the border of Judea and Israel, in Ephraim, or on the border between Phoenicia, Israel, and Aram? The poet's geographical additions to the book of Jonah produce a figure migrant between lands. Geographical indetermination continues to the present day: what was the region of Ephraim is still in the midst of Israeli territory. The spine of the Hermon mountain range lies between Lebanon and Syria. From its highest peak there are views of Israel, Jordan, Amman, the West Bank, and the Golan Heights.

The final location that the poet introduces is Samaria (116). Jonah believes that when he has gone from there God will not see him. As the maps in Appendix E show, in the Old Testament Samaria was a town. In the New Testament, Samaria has become a region separate from Judea. The geographic diaspora of place names emphasizes how far from home God asks Jonah to travel. He is isolated from his "kyth" (462), a word used also for family and derived from Old English *cuþ* [what is known]. On the boat, destined for Tarshish, Jonah is among strangers who do not speak his language (213). The detail is present in the source, but along with the poet's geographical additions, it emphasizes Jonah's estrangement. The introduction of place names that are not present in the Book of Jonah also serve to highlight Jonah's uniqueness as a prophet. Only he, of all the Old Testament prophets, preaches to people who are not Jews. Only Jonah preaches to people who are not of his own race. Consciously or not, the *Patience*-poet creates a scenario in which God's commands to his prophet turn him into a type of crusader. In the late fourteenth century, crusades were a hot topic of contention. Wycliffites condemned the practice; Chaucer fudges the issue in his ambiguous description of the Knight in the *General Prologue to the Canterbury Tales*.

The biographical geography of *Patience* reproduces a historical tangle of territorial appropriation. Between the Old and New Testaments, and to writing at the present, control over locations changes hands repeatedly. Nineveh, for instance, was once the capital of the Assyrian empire. Under the emperor Sennacherib, Nineveh became a magnificent city (c. 700 BCE). Sennacherib built a resplendent palace with at least eighty rooms, many of them lined with sculpture. In 612 BCE, however, Nineveh suffered a defeat from which it never recovered: Babylonians, Scythians, and Medes sacked the city; it was reduced to ash. Excavations in the 1840s by the Englishman Henry Layard (1817–94) confirmed the splendour of the palace buried under rubble. Its glorious sculptures were shipped off to Canford Magna in Dorset (the home of Layard's sponsor, John Guest [1785–1852]), before being sent to the British Museum, where they are still on display. Canford Magna subsequently became a public boarding school, and in 1992, a piece of the sculptures thought to have been missing was discovered in the tuck shop, painted over with vinyl emulsion. Restored, though with some residual pockmarks as a result of having been positioned near a dartboard, it fetched £7 million from Japanese bidders at auction. A new school house was built, and every child in the school received a Mars bar.

While in *Patience* and the biblical book of Jonah, Nineveh survives destruction, the later Old Testament Book of Nahum speaks of its annihilation with unrestrained jubilance. Three chapters detail the luxurious sins of the Assyrians: their extravagance, their relish for merchandise, and rich commodities in silver and gold. Nahum prophesies that the name of Nineveh will be lost, and God will make its pagan images its grave, for the people are vile. Nahum tells of a furious, vengeful God whose way is in whirlwind and storm. He will dry up the seas and the rivers, melting the hills to restore the majesty of Israel against its plunderers. God's threats are far more virulent than in *Patience*. He promises that he will lift up the skirts of Nineveh so that all nations can gaze on its nakedness; he will throw filth at the people and treat them with contempt and make them a laughing stock. All peoples shall shrink from contact with Ninevites, and there will be no one to mourn the city's waste (Nahum 3:5–7).

Retrospectively, Jonah is proved right; Nahum's God is terrifying in his capacity for destruction.

And before we leave the pride and fall of Nineveh, it might be salutary to note that Jonah was a prophet not only in the Judeo-Christian tradition. The *Qur'an*, Chapter 10, records the prophecy of Yunus, the Islamic Jonah (see Appendix A4). The Muslim prophet Yunus is known also as "Dhun-Nun" (Lord of the Fish) and "Sahibil-Hot" (Companion of the Fish). Jonah/Yunus was remembered with honour for his preaching: a mosque on the site of Nineveh built by the Ayyubids in 1226 is believed to contain Jonah's shrine and a tooth from the whale that swallowed him. The Tomb of Yunus, one of Iraq's iconic monuments, sits on a mound that contains many layers of history: an ancient Assyrian temple and palace, a site of devotion for Jews, a Christian church, and a thirteenth-century mosque. The tomb was renovated in the 1990s under Saddam Hussein (1937–2006). On 24 July 2014, in an attack by ISIS on Mosul, the Tomb of Yunus was destroyed.

Samaria's history is no less interesting. After its defeat by the king of the Assyrians, it was, according to one Old Testament author, repopulated with "foreign nations ignorant of the ordinances of the Lord," who sent lions to punish them (2 Kings 17:26). Samaria is a byword for sin (Ezekiel 16:51), the site of pagan temples and devilish practices (1 Kings 16:32; 2 Kings 1:3). It is full of falsehood (Hosea 7:1), and its prophets deceive the people of Israel (Jeremiah 23:13). Hostility between Jews and Samaritans continues in the New Testament, but with a twist. When the Woman of Samaria meets Jesus at Jacob's Well and he asks her to drink, she replies, "[h]ow dost thou, being a Jew, ask of me to drink, who am a Samaritan woman? For the Jews do not communicate with the Samaritans" (John 4:10). But, despite her marital sins, she does drink, repents of her iniquity, and proceeds to spread Jesus' teachings among the Samaritans. Luke tells two parables concerning Samaritans. First, the story of the Good Samaritan (Luke 10:31–37) compares the indifferent callousness of a priest and a Levite toward a wounded man dying by the roadside with the compassion of the Samaritan who stops to help and to heal him. Second, Chapter 17 records the miracle in which Jesus heals ten lepers. Only one of them thanks him: "he fell on his face before his feet, giving thanks: and this was a Samaritan. And Jesus answering, said, Were not ten made clean? and where are the nine? There is no one found to return and give glory to God, but this stranger" (Luke 17:17–19). Jesus, a Jew, is compassionate toward the foreigners of Samaria. In return, those whom he heals, or who show compassion to a stranger themselves, are exalted in comparison to the Jews.

The inclusion of Samaria in *Patience* (116) is not strictly necessary to secure alliteration: the poet could easily have rendered the line "That gone from His *sight* [or *Israel*], God couldn't see him." Whatever the reasons for the addition, the poet plants a tiny poetic time capsule in his poem that captures the explosiveness of tensions between regions of the Middle East—and the possibility for overriding them. When the reference to Samaria is unpacked, we are made aware that a group of foreigners, once demonized for their different religious practices, are shown to be merciful and kind to those who stereotyped them in the first place. It is hard for a twenty-first-century reader (or me, at any rate) not to notice that the biographical geography of *Patience* records centuries of fear, mistrust, hostility, and appropriation of possessions, beliefs, and land. Despite the possibilities of redemption offered by the recuperation of the reputation of Samarians, the geography of *Patience* predicts centuries of such intransigent cultural volatility that to draw any maps to represent the territory of the poem, past or present, becomes a cartographical minefield.

A Note on Translation

Patience is written in alliterative metre. This is a verse form much closer to Old English than the rhymed verse influenced by Continental models and used by authors such as Geoffrey Chaucer (c. 1343–1400) and John Gower (c. 1330–1408). As Chaucer's Parson attests, "[b]ut trusteþ wel I am a suthren man / I can not geste / Rum, raf, ruf by letter" (*Canterbury Tales*, X.420–43), this verse form was associated with northern writing. When *Patience* was written there was no standardized form of English. The diversity of dialects was chiefly geographical, and poets (and scribes) wrote in their native dialects. Alliterative metre was used chiefly in the southwest, the west Midlands, and the northwest, though, as *Piers Plowman* shows, alliterative metre was also deployed by poets whose origins may have been in one of these areas but were writing in London. It is possible that the poet of Cotton Nero MS A.x was attached to an aristocratic court whose nobility spent some time in London.

An alliterative line had an a-verse and a b-verse that were linked by alliteration on the initial letters of words which carried strong metrical stress. This was the basic template, as in, for instance, "I schal **t**ee into **T**arce and **t**ary þere a whyle" (87). The a-verse often had two alliterative staves; the b-verse had one. There were many variations on this pattern, however. The a-verse could be extended with three alliterative staves, often, though not always, in particularly dramatic passages, such as "Ro3 rakkes þer ros with rudnyng anvnder; / Þe see sou3ed ful sore, gret selly to here" (139–40). Lines might also have four alliterative staves, two in each half-verse, which emphasize sensory content, as in "He **gl**ydes in by þe **g**iles þur3 **gl**aym ande **gl**ette" (269).

Sometimes, when the tone is lighter, a line may have just two alliterative staves: "**L**orde, to Þe haf I **cl**eped in **c**arez ful stronge" (305). As in line 269, the alliterative staves are a mix of initial letter and consonant cluster (*cl* and *c*). There is also a second acoustic pattern in line 305 using the sound [l] ("Lorde," "cleped," and "ful"). Some lines carry alliteration on strong and weak stresses, as in "Bi þe **h**aspede **h**e **h**entes **h**ym þenne" (189); pronouns carry alliterative freight alongside nouns and verbs. The number of unstressed syllables between staves varies hugely. We might compare line 189 with a later line that also alliterates on the sound [h]: "For nade þe **h**y3e **H**euen-Kyng, þur3 **H**is **h**onde my3t" (257). Words with initial [h] also alliterated with vowels. Line 2, "When **h**euy **h**erttes ben **h**urt wyth **h**eþyng **o**þer **e**lles," e.g., has five alliterative staves.

At times, the poet may continue an alliterative pattern in consecutive lines. This is characteristic of the lines that recount the Beatitudes:

> A3t **h**appes **H**e **h**em **h**y3t and vcheon a mede,
> **S**underlupes, for hit **d**issert, vpon a **s**er **w**yse:
> Thay **a**rn **h**appen þat **h**an in **h**ert pouerte,
> For **h**ores is þe **h**euen-ryche to **h**olde for **e**uer;
> Þay **a**r **h**appen also þat **h**aunte mekenesse. (11–15)

Four of these lines alliterate on [h] or on vowels. Line 12, by contrast, is of a different rhythm entirely, with an alliterative stave that starts the line, a consonant cluster in the middle of the noun ("dissert"), an alliterating adverb ("ser"), and sibilance in the first and last words. Even in the lines that have [h] and vowel alliteration, the number of syllables, the positions of stresses, and the presence or absence of a medial caesura creates a rhythmical texture that is constantly in flux. Compare line 11, with its caesura and with strong stress on "mede," with the absence of a caesura and the weakly stressed final three syllables "mekenesse" in line 15.

Alliterative metre is no longer a major verse form. With the process of standardization and the advent of the printing press, alliterative verse fell out of fashion. Shakespeare satirizes alliterating verse through the character of Bottom in the artisans' play in *A Midsummer Night's Dream* (1595). George Puttenham (c. 1529–91), in his *Arte of English Poesie* (1589), describes alliteration as "tautologia or self-saying" which has nothing to commend it, especially if it is overused, such as when a maker takes too much delight to fill his verse with words all beginning with the same letter. Nonetheless, alliteration has been used by major poets: Walt Whitman (1819–92) in *Leaves of Grass* (1855); Edgar Allan Poe (1809–49) in *The Raven* (1845); the poems of Gerard Manley Hopkins (1844–89); or *The Age of Anxiety* (1948) by W.H. Auden (1907–73). Having once been a significant metrical form, however, alliteration has assumed the lesser status of a device or embellishment. Its most common use is in advertising—"naughty but nice" (Salman Rushdie on cream cakes)—and political slogans: "a future fair for all" (UK General Election 2010) or "strong and stable leadership" (UK General Election 2017). Headline writers also delight in alliteration: "Mysterious metal monolith disappears from Utah desert" *(ABC News* 2022).

My translation attempts to fuse the practice of Middle English alliterative poetry with an acoustic verse that feels less like a translation and more like a new poem. I retain all the alliterative patterns used in *Patience* and introduce some variations. The majority of lines have two stressed alliterative staves in the a-verse and one in the b-verse, e.g., lines 1–5 and 272–77. There are lines that have three alliterative staves in the a-verse, e.g., lines 221, 298, and 495. Some lines have one alliterating stave in the a-verse and two in the b-verse, e.g., lines 66, 82, and 468. Many lines embellish alliteration with four alliterating staves, e.g., lines 1, 42, 93, 136, 151, 311, 513, and 531. I have also used the practice of double alliteration where there are two alliterating patterns in a line, e.g., [b] and [f], line 340; [w] and [t], line 358; and [k] and [m], line 396.

The alliteration falls chiefly on initial consonants or vowels, but I have also followed the practice in *Patience* of alliterating initial and medial sounds, e.g., "With your **tr**eacherous **tr**icks to des**tr**oy us all" (198). Some lines mix initial and terminal alliterative sounds, e.g., "What you've do**n**e's been **n**oticed. Your **n**umber's up!" (203), and one line alliterates solely on medial and terminal sounds; to have done otherwise would have destroyed the plangency of the line "All me**n**, wome**n**, childre**n** and a**n**imals" (388). The repetition of [n] provides an additional acoustic pattern. Furthermore, in order to sustain idiomatic Modern English, I have occasionally plundered the possibilities afforded by elision between a consonant and a vowel, e.g., "**N**o way you're going to **N**ineveh, the**n**, **e**h?" (346) and "Though that shrimp **in** his **p**aunch was **p**esky—I'm sure" (299). Line 299 also illustrates my practice of providing a secondary acoustic pattern if there are only two strong alliterative staves—in this instance sibilance, and assonance between "paunch" and "sure." Assonance, dissonance, and half rhyme have also been used to secure a strong heartbeat in the poem, e.g., in lines 2, 37, 74, 174, 260, 281, 332, 361–63, 437–40, and 453–55. As in *Patience*, there is a huge variety in the number of unstressed syllables in the lines, for instance "All hope lost he calls to his Lord" (281) and "With all the mayhem you can muster, molest me endlessly" (484).

The dynamic catalogue passages depend as much on syntax as on vocabulary and metrical rhythm to create their drama. So, in the sailors' labours to ready their ship (102–08), or in the descriptions of the storm (137–60), I have tried to mirror the syntax as well as to find appropriate diction. The poet varies the speed of his poem. Some of the standalone lines, or half-lines, orchestrate the poem's humour (e.g., 280 and 460). I have attempted to retain this kinesis, and also in sections of the poem where much shorter lines punctuate the narrative, either to comment on the action or to recreate sudden reversals or unexpected outcomes in the action, especially, but not only, when these are performed by God (e.g., 406 and 442–44). Compared with the Middle English verse form, I have introduced many lines which end with a final alliterative stave. Apart from lines in the traditional alliterative staple that create fluent English, there is much less frequent use of a caesura mid-line. The rhythm of my translation sounds different from that in *Patience*. There is more enjambement between lines. I have tried to produce a poem in alliterative metre (rather than a poem that uses alliteration), but to score the Middle English alliterative line to more contemporary ears.

Middle English alliterative verse uses a wealth of synonyms to create alliterative staves. Much of this vocabulary is no longer used in standardized English, for instance: "swelme" (3); "þro, þole" (6); "waltered" (142); "no tytter outtulde" (231); "kark" (265); "bygge" (302); "spakly" (338); "wlonk" (486); and "luþer" (500). "Word for word" translation would have been impossible, even if that had been my aim. However, some Middle English words are still used widely in spoken varieties of English, especially "thole," meaning "to suffer" (Northern and Scottish). I have retained "thole" in lines 6 and 521. Not every reader of Middle English poetry is a standard English speaker.

On the same principle, I have used regional varieties of English to translate other alliterative staves. From northern English: "gob" (199); "jip" (241); "jiggered" (488); and "cack" (279). From Scottish or Northern Irish: "thran" (6) and "gurn" (372, 433). From US slang: "guff" (66) and "barf" (340). Some readers may find the colloquialism of some lines in my translation displeasing, but I have retained dialect variety and slang, even some taboo vocabulary—e.g., "shit" (275)—to reproduce the significant changes in register in *Patience*. Hence "lump it" (42); "guv'nor" (199); "chunter" (54); "stir your stumps" (65); "suss" (127); "bloke" (276); and "piffle" (428). And I have not shied away from translating archaic idioms into more contemporary English: "two peas in a pod" (37); "your number's up" (203); "walk the plank" (204); "lets rip" (410); "both barrels" (411); and "skint," "in a scrape," and "hit the skids" (528).

One crucial aspect of the register of the Middle English text that is impossible to reproduce without significant distortion of tone is the use of interpersonal pronouns. In Middle English, the "you" pronoun was used as it still is in many Continental languages (and in varieties of British and American English). That is, there is a distinction between the second-person singular "thou, thee, thy, and thine," and plural "you, your, and yours." Alongside differentiating between singular and plural, the "you" form of the pronoun was used by an inferior to their superior, for instance, between a servant and their master, and the "thou" form was used between friends, intimates, or by a master to their servant. The choice of pronoun was a sign of the power relations between two persons: equal, superior, or inferior. That distinction has been lost in Modern Standard English but was a crucial marker of status in written texts before its standardization.

The poet of *Patience* was well aware of this distinction, as we see in *Sir Gawain and the Green Knight* when Gawain addresses King Arthur (343–61), or in *Pearl*, when the dreamer apologizes to the Pearl maiden for his rudeness but vacillates uncertainly between the polite and intimate forms of "thou" and "you" (385–96 and 913–18). The only usage of "you" in *Patience* is to mark addressees in the plural (212; 362; 385). We would expect God to use the "thou" pronoun when speaking to Jonah. We might expect the sailors to use the same pronoun to address a wretched stowaway whose presence on board has wrecked their ship and threatened their lives. More surprising is the fact that Jonah uses the "thou" pronoun to God. That is, Jonah addresses God as if he were his intimate or his equal. To use the "thou" pronoun in a modern English translation does not capture this imbalance of power. Outside dialect usage, "thou" in written texts is reserved chiefly for archaism in poetry or to address God, or another religious deity, with respect. For this reason, I have not capitalized Jonah's usage of "you" toward God, as it introduces a note of reverence that the text conspicuously lacks.

To have effaced this crucial interpersonal dynamic in the poem would have misrepresented the poet's craft. Jonah's presumption ought to sound shocking, so I have used a blunt colloquial register for Jonah's speeches to God, and also God's to Jonah. The same principle guides my translation of the sailors' speeches to Jonah, and also of some sections in the narrator's voice. While *Patience* is a written text, its handling of poetic voice articulates the difficult theological questions the poem raises, and also the close attention to felt human experience and to sensory detail. I have wanted to capture voice in my translation, not just to try to bring the poem to life but also because I think the vocal performances in *Patience* are integral to its work.

There are often marked changes in register: the shift from the anaphoric reverential narration of the Beatitudes to the narrator's lewd gloss on the ninth blessing he conjures from the biblical text (13–30; 31–45). Words of Latinate or French register are used densely in Jonah's prayers to God from the whale's belly (284–88; 325–29), after the desolation of his woodbine (417–20), and in the speech of the king of the Ninevites (396–401). I have tried to match my register accordingly to recreate the shift in tone. The poet also uses syntactic modulation to create a similar effect. The blunt, short questions of the mariners create a curt abruptness that contrasts with both Jonah's measured explanation of his origins and mission and his recounting of God's creation (196–204; 205–12).

I have wanted to try to produce a poem which, while faithful to Middle English sense and style, could be read on its own terms by a twenty-first-century readership, and not necessarily a readership that is exclusively, or professionally, academic. The notes to my translation give literal readings of diction, idioms, and embellishments so that readers who wish to do so can navigate between source text and translation and judge for themselves whether my rendition does the job of the lines as they read them. And apart from some knotty points of translation (especially the opening and closing lines), I have not provided a detailed reasoning for where I have knowingly departed from what I believe to be a more literal rendering of the poem. *Patience* is a poem that makes us think. It doesn't nanny us with answers. To my mind, it would disrespect the poem to attempt to carapace it with a rigid commentary that sucks all the life from the poet's rambunctious craft. Cole Porter puts it perfectly: "Jonah made his home in / A whale's abdomen. *It ain't necessarily so!*"

A Note on the Text

I have presented a conservative edition based on the facsimile produced by Sir Israel Gollancz for the Early English Text Society. As *Patience* exists in a single copy, I have emended manuscript readings only when there is obvious sign of error and the line makes no sense as it stands. There are only a few places in the poem where this occurs, and I have followed the practice of previous editors in making minor adjustments. I have not introduced any emendations on metrical grounds. Straightforward emendations, with a long editorial history, are simply noted at the foot of the page of the Middle English text, e.g., line 35, "fyn" emended to "syn." More complex issues—for instance, whether there has been transposition of lines in 509–15, where God's voice ends in the poem, and the inclusion of the word "nobel" (531)—are discussed in the notes to the text and translation. Spelling conventions follow those of the edition of *Patience* in J.A. Burrow and Thorlac Turville-Petre, *A Book of Middle English*. I keep the Middle English grapheme <þ> (thorn). This is equivalent to Modern English <th>, for example in "Þen ay þrow forth my þro, þaȝ me þynk ylle" (8). I also retain <ȝ> (yogh) when it represents either <y> in initial position or <gh> in medial position, for example in "And al to lyȝten þat lome, ȝif leþe wolde schape" (160). The letters <u/v> and <i/j> are regularized to conform to modern usage, and throughout, contractions such as "&" are silently expanded. Capitalization and punctuation are editorial.

PATIENCE

Pacience

[f83ʳ] Pacience is a poynt, þaȝ hit displese ofte.
When heuy herttes ben hurt wyth heþyng oþer elles,
Suffraunce may aswagen hem and þe swelme leþe,
For ho quelles uche a qued and quenches malice,
5   For quoso suffer cowþe syt, sele wolde folȝe,
And quo for þro may noȝt þole, þe þikker he sufferes.
Þen is better to abyde þe bur umbestoundes
Þen ay þrow forth my þro, þaȝ me þynk ylle.
I herde on a halyday, at a hyȝe masse,
10 How Mathew melede þat his Mayster His meyny con teche.
Aȝt happes He hem hyȝt and ucheon a mede,
Sunderlupes, for hit dissert, upon a ser wyse:
Thay arn happen þat han in hert poverte,
For hores is þe heven-ryche to holde for ever;
15 Þay ar happen also þat haunte mekenesse,
For þay schal welde þis worlde and alle her wylle have;
Thay ar happen also þat for her harme wepes,
For þay schal comfort encroche in kythes ful mony;
Þay ar happen also þat hungeres after ryȝt,
20 For þay schal frely be refete ful of alle gode;
Thay ar happen also þat han in hert rauþe,
For mercy in alle maneres her mede schal worþe;
Þay ar happen also þat arn of hert clene,
For þay her Savyour in sete schal se with her yȝen;
25 Thay ar happen also þat halden her pese,
For þay þe gracious Godes sunes schal godly be called;
Þay ar happen also þat con her hert stere,
For hores is þe heven-ryche, as I er sayde.
These arn þe happes alle aȝt þat uus bihyȝt weren,
30 If we þyse ladyes wolde lof in lyknyng of þewes:
[f83ᵛ] Dame Povert, Dame Pitée, Dame Penaunce þe þrydde
Dame Mekenesse, Dame Mercy, and miry Clannesse,
And þenne Dame Pes, and Pacyence put in þerafter.
He were happen þat hade one; alle were þe better.
35 Bot syn I am put to a poynt þat poverté hatte,
I schal me porvay pacyence and play me with boþe,
For in þe tyxte þere þyse two arn in teme layde,
Hit arn fettled in on forme, þe forme and þe laste,

---

3. aswagen] MS aswagend
35. syn] MS fyn

Translation

Patience is a pip that's often unpleasant.
Hearts, hassel backed with harm or hurt,
Are assuaged and soothed if you suffer the broil,
All conflict and rancour is completely quelled,
If you can sit with sorrow, solace will follow, 5
If you're thran when you should thole, you'll get thrashed.
I'm better to bear the odd bad blow,
Than endlessly lament my resentment.
I heard on a Holy Day, at a High Mass,
What Matthew said his Master taught His men. 10
Eight outcomes He promised, each one a reward,
Awarded to each in accord with what they'd earned.
Blessed are those whose hearts are humble,
They shall have keys to the Kingdom for keeps.
Blessed also are those who abide obedience, 15
They shall govern this globe and get their desires.
Blessed also are the weepers, wretched with woes,
They shall have healing in their several homelands.
Blessed also are those who thirst after justice,
They shall graciously be given all good things. 20
Blessed also are those whose hearts are compassionate,
Mercy shall reward them; wide open-armed.
Blessed also the pure: pearls polished clean,
They shall gaze on their Saviour seated on high.
Blessed also the quiet who curb their rancour, 25
They shall be called God's children in charity.
Blessed also are those who rule their wrath with reason,
They shall have heaven—as I said a little earlier.
These are all the eight blessings we were assured,
If we love the blameless lives of these ladies: 30
Dame Poverty, Dame Pity, Dame Penance the third,
Dame Meekness, Dame Mercy, and merry Dame Purity,
And keep a place warm for Dames Patience and Peace.
To have one of them is a blessing, though better to have them all!
But since I'm supposed to be saddled with Poverty 35
I'll make Patience my mistress and be merry with both.
In the Bible, these "P"s are two peas in a pod,
They come as a package, a pair you can't part,

And by quest of her quoyntyse enquylen on mede.
40 And als, in myn upynyoun, hit arn of on kynde:
For þeras povert hir proferes ho nyl be put utter,
Bot lenge wheresoever hir lyst, lyke oþer greme;
And þereas povert enpresses, þaȝ mon pyne þynk,
Much, maugré his mun, he mot nede suffer;
45 Thus poverté and pacyence arn nedes playferes.
Syþen I am sette with hem samen, suffer me byhoves;
Þenne is me lyȝtloker hit lyke and her lotes prayse,
Þenne wyþer wyth and be wroth and þe wers have.
Ȝif me be dyȝt a destyné due to have,
50 What dowes me þe dedayn, oþer dispit make?
Oþer ȝif my lege lorde lyst on lyve me to bidde
Oþer to ryde oþer to renne to Rome in his ernde,
What grayþed me þe grychchyng bot grame more seche?
Much if he me ne made, maugref my chekes,
55 And þenne þrat moste I þole and unþonk to mede,
Þe had bowed to his bode bongré my hyure.
Did not Jonas in Judé suche jape sumwhyle?
To sette hym to sewrté, unsounde he hym feches.
Wyl ȝe tary a lyttel tyne and tent me a whyle,
60 I schal wysse yow þerwyth as holy wryt telles.
Hit bitydde sumtyme in þe termes of Judé,
Jonas joyned watz þerinne Jentyle prophete;
Goddes glam to hym glod þat hym unglad made,
With a roghlych rurd rowned in his ere:
65 "Rys radly," He says, "And rayke forth even
[f84ʳ] Nym þe way to Nynyve wythouten oþer speche
And in þat ceté My saȝes soghe alle aboute,
Þat in þat place, at þe poynt, I put in þi hert.
For iwysse hit arn so wykke þat in þat won dowellez
70 And her malys is so much, I may not abide
Bot venge Me on her vilanye and venym bilyve;
Now sweȝe Me þider swyftly and say Me þis arende."
When þat steven watz stynt þat stowned his mynde,
Al he wrathed in his wyt, and wyþerly he þoȝt:
75 "If I bowe to His bode and bryng hem þis tale,
And I be nummen in Nunive, my nyes begynes:
He telles me þose traytoures arn typped schrewes;
I com wyth þose tyþynges, þay ta me bylyve,
Pynez me in a prysoun, put me in stokkes,

---

73. stowned] MS stownod

To seek their wisdom wins you one reward.
Essentially, I own, they are one and the same, 40
If Poverty pokes her nose in, she'll not be pushed out,
She'll linger where she likes, like it or lump it.
And Poverty's oppressive, thought to be a pain,
She'll make your life a misery however much you moan:
Poverty and Patience are inseparable playmates. 45
Since I'm landed with them both I'll have to live with them,
Better to tolerate them and to extol their charms
Than resist them angrily and fetch up more wretched.
If I find I'm to follow a path that is fixed
What do I gain if I grumble and grouch? 50
If my superior decides to assign me a task,
Riding or running to Rome at his bidding,
It's no good my grizzling; I'd just get more grief.
Fat chance he'll change his mind though I chunter,
I'd be forced, paid back with disfavour, 55
When I ought to have obeyed him in accord with my hire.
There's a jape about Jonah who lived in Judea—
Who fell flat on his face as he tried to play safe.
If you'll linger a little, and listen to me,
I'll tell you the tale as it's told in the Bible. 60
A long while ago in the land of Judea
When Jonah was picked for the Gentiles' prophet,
With vim, God's voice vroomed right in his ear,
Rough, and gruff, it rattled his drum.
"Stir your stumps swiftly, and set out at once, 65
Go to Nineveh (and don't give me guff!)
Spread my speeches throughout the city,
I'll teach you what words to say—and when to do so.
Its denizens be so devilish debauched
I can no longer live with their malevolence, 70
I must revenge their venomous evil at once.
Get you gone then and give them my message."
When the speaking stopped, Jonah was stunned,
His wits in a tizz, resistant; worrying that
"If I cave to his commands and convey these words 75
And I'm kidnapped in Nineveh, I'm done for.
He tells me those traitors are top-notch thugs,
If I arrive with those instructions, they'll arrest me:
Plonk me in prison or place me in stocks,

80 Wryþe me in a warlok, wrast out myn y3en.
Þis is a mervayl message a man for to preche
Amonge enmyes so mony and mansed fendes,
Bot if my gaynlych God such gref to me wolde,
For desert of sum sake þat I slayn were.
85 At alle peryles," quoþ þe prophete, "I aproche hit no nerre.
I wyl me sum oþer waye þat He ne wayte after;
I schal tee into Tarce and tary þere a whyle,
And ly3tly when I am lest He letes me alone."
Þenne he ryses radly and raykes bilyve,
90 Jonas toward port Japh, ay janglande for tene
Þat he nolde þole for noþyng non of þose pynes,
Þa3 þe Fader þat hym formed were fale of his hele.
"Oure Syre syttes," he says, "on sege so hy3e
In His glowande glorye, and gloumbes ful lyttel
95 Þa3 I be nummen in Nunnive and naked dispoyled,
On rode rwly torent with rybaudes mony."
Þus he passes to þat port his passage to seche,
Fyndes he a fayr schyp to þe fare redy,
Maches hym with þe maryneres, makes her paye
100 For to towe hym into Tarce as tyd as þay my3t.
Then he tron on þo tres, and þay her tramme ruchen,
Cachen vp þe crossayl, cables þay fasten,
[f84ᵛ] Wi3t at þe wyndas we3en her ankres,
Spende spak to þe sprete þe spare bawelyne,
105 Gederen to þe gyde-ropes, þe grete cloþ falles,
Þay layden in on laddeborde, and þe lofe wynnes,
Þe blyþe breþe at her bak þe bosum he fyndes;
He swenges me þys swete schip swefte fro þe haven.
Watz never so joyful a Jue as Jonas watz þenne,
110 Þat þe daunger of Dry3tyn so derfly ascaped;
He wende wel þat þat Wy3 þat al þe world planted
Hade no ma3t in þat mere no man for to greve.
Lo, þe wytles wrechche! For he wolde no3t suffer,
Now hatz he put hym in plyt of peril wel more.
115 Hit watz a wenyng unwar þat welt in his mynde,
Þa3 he were so3t fro Samarye, þat God ses no fyrre.
3ise, He blusched ful brode: þat burde hym by sure;
Þat ofte kyd hym þe carpe þat kyng sayde,

---

84. For] MS fof
94. glowande] MS g wande (nothing legible in space between g and w)

Declare me a devil and dig out my eyes. 80
That's a marvellous message for a man to preach
To a hostile crowd, in hock to hell!
Unless my gracious God plans such grief for me,
That I'm killed to correct some crime?
Happen what may," he said, "I'll mind my back, 85
I'll go by other ground He does not guard,
Slink off to Tarshish and skulk there a while,
When I'm lost He'll likely leave me alone."
Jonah springs up sprightly and speeds his way
To the port of Joppa, each step a protest, 90
There's no way he'd endure even one of those wrongs
If the Father who formed him can't be faffed to look after him.
"Our Lord lounges aloof on His lofty perch,
Glowing in glory, and wouldn't give a damn
Were I nabbed in Nineveh and stripped naked 95
On a cross, sharked shamefully by a crew of scum."
He proceeds to the port to procure his passage
And spies a fine ship, ready to sail,
Shakes hands with the sailors and settles in cash
To ship him to Tarshish—sharpish! 100
He dawdles on deck while they deal with their gear,
Raise the main-sail, secure the ropes,
Lasso the windlass with the anchor weights,
Bind the bow-line tight to the bowsprit,
Haul on harnesses to hold the huge sheet, 105
Ply their oars port-side to profit from the wind
That swirls at the stern to swell the sails and
Blows the blessed boat fast from the port.
Never then was there Jew as joyful as Jonah,
Tickled pink with his trick to escape the Lord's threat, 110
He knew all too well God grew only the earth,
No power to punish on the open sea.
Honestly, what an idiot! For want of endurance
He's dumped in more danger, the direst of straits!
His mind seized by the stupid assumption 115
That gone from Samaria, God couldn't see him.
But God sees all things as Jonah should have known:
He'd taught him the text that the Psalmist spoke,

  Dyngne David on des þat demed þis speche
120 In a psalme þat he set þe sauter withinne:
  "O folez in folk, felez oþerwhyle
  And understondes umbestounde, þa3 3e be stape in folé,
  Hope 3e þat He heres not þat eres alle made?
  Hit may not be þat He is blynde þat bigged uche y3e."
125 Bot he dredes no dynt þat dotes for elde.
  For he watz fer in þe flod foundande to Tarce,
  Bot I trow ful tyd overtan þat he were,
  So þat schomely to schort he schote of his ame.
  For þe Welder of wyt þat wot alle þynges,
130 Þat ay wakes and waytes, at wylle hatz He sly3tes.
  He calde on þat ilk crafte He carf with His hondes;
  Þay wakened wel þe wroþeloker for wroþely He cleped:
  "Ewrus and Aquiloun þat on est sittes
  Blowes boþe at My bode upon blo watteres."
135 Þenne watz no tom þer bytwene His tale and her dede,
  So bayn wer þay boþe two His bone for to wyrk.
  Anon out of þe norþ-est þe noys bigynes,
  When boþe breþes con blowe upon blo watteres.
[f85ʳ] Ro3 rakkes þer ros with rudnyng anunder;
140 Þe see sou3ed ful sore, gret selly to here;
  Þe wyndes on þe wonne water so wrastel togeder
  Þat þe wawes ful wode waltered so hi3e
  And efte busched to þe abyme, þat breed fysches
  Durst nowhere for ro3 arest at þe bothem.
145 When þe breth and þe brok and þe bote metten,
  Hit watz a joyles gyn þat Jonas watz inne,
  For hit reled on roun upon þe ro3e yþes.
  Þe bur ber to hit baft, þat braste alle her gere,
  Þen hurled on a hepe þe helme and þe sterne;
150 Furst tomurte mony rop and þe mast after;
  Þe sayl sweyed on þe see, þenne suppe bihoved
  Þe coge of þe colde water, and þenne þe cry ryses.
  3et corven þay þe cordes and kest al þeroute;
  Mony ladde þer forth lep to lave and to kest,
155 Scopen out þe scaþel water þat fayn scape wolde,

---

122. 3e] MS he
122. in] MS om
152. colde] MS clolde

In dignity on his dais, David declared these words
From a psalm he had set down in his Psalter: 120
"O foolish folk, fettle your thoughts for once,
And mark, though you maze in mad surmise.
How could He who made all ears be unable to hear!
Or He who devised eyes be unable to see?
Only those in their dotage dread no disaster ahead!"   125
Convinced he's invisible, he cruises to Tarshish,
Too slow to suss he'd been spied from the start,
But he shot shamefully short of his intended mark.
Nothing escapes the notice of Omniscient God,
Never asleep, He has tricks up His sleeve.   130
He calls out to His creation He crafted by hand:
They awake the angrier; for He orders in wrath.
"Eurus and Aquilon, you live in the East,
Whip up your winds on the waters' dark waves."
No sooner said than the summons was sped,   135
So obedient were both to begin his command.
Cacophonous noise erupts from the north,
Once both blow their breath across the black waters.
Rough storm clouds arise raddled with red,
The sea howls in pain, horrendous to hear.   140
The winds wrestle so fiercely with the water's force
That the furious sea soars to unsurpassed heights,
And then plunges to the pit so that petrified fish,
Don't dare dwell in the depths of the deep.
When the winds and the waves wrangle together,   145
Jonah's truculence turns treacherous trap:
The ship rears its head through the rough heaving waves,
Bludgeoned backwards, the sea-tackle bursts,
The tiller and the rudder could not be told apart.
The ropes unravelled first, then the mast was wrecked,   150
The sinking sail forced to swallow sea,
Cold waves clog the boat. The sailors cry out,
Cut all cords free and cast them overboard.
All hands on deck ditch dirt overboard,
Scoop out sewage, frantic to escape   155

For be monnes lode never so luþer, þe lyf is ay swete.
Þer watz busy over borde bale to kest,
Her bagges and her feþer-beddes and her bryȝt wedes,
Her kysttes and her coferes, her caraldes alle,
160 And al to lyȝten þat lome, ȝif leþe wolde schape.
Bot ever watz ilyche loud þe lot of þe wyndes,
And ever wroþer þe water and wodder þe stremes.
Þen þo wery forwroȝt wyst no bote,
Bot uchon glewed on his god þat gayned hym beste:
165 Summe to Vernagu þer vouched avowes solemne,
Summe to Diana devout and derf Neptune,
To Mahoun and to Mergot, þe mone and þe sunne,
And uche lede as he loved and layde had his hert.
Þenne bispeke þe spakest, dispayred wel nere:
170 "I leve here be sum losynger, sum lawles wrech,
Þat hatz greved his god and gotz here amonge uus.
Lo, al synkes in his synne and for his sake marres.
I lovue þat we lay lotes on ledes uchone,
And whoso lympes þe losse, lay hym þeroute;
[f85ᵛ] 175 And quen þe gulty is gon, what may gome trawe
Bot He þat rules þe rak may rwe on þose oþer?"
Þis watz sette in asent, and sembled þay were,
Herȝed out of uche hyrne to hent þat falles.
A lodesmon lyȝtly lep under hachches,
180 For to layte mo ledes and hem to lote bryng.
Bot hym fayled no freke þat he fynde myȝt,
Saf Jonas þe Jwe, þat jowked in derne.
He watz flowen for ferde of þe flode lotes
Into þe boþem of þe bot, and on a brede lyggede,
185 Onhelde by þe hurrok, for þe heven wrache,
Slypped upon a sloumbe-selepe, and sloberande he routes.
Þe freke hym frunt with his fot and bede hym ferk up:
Þer Ragnel in his rakentes hym rere of his dremes!
Bi þe haspede he hentes hym þenne,
190 And broȝt hym up by þe brest and upon borde sette,
Arayned hym ful runyschly what raysoun he hade
In such slaȝtes of sorȝe to slepe so faste.
Sone haf þay her sortes sette and serelych deled,
And ay þe lote upon laste lymped on Jonas.

---

194. þe] MS þe þe

(However hard one's life is, existence is dear).
They bustle to empty the boat of its burden:
Finery, feather beds, and fashionable clothes,
Caskets, coffers, precious crafted boxes,
To lighten the ship should lee be allowed them. 160
But the winds won't rest from their deafening roars,
The waves ever wilder, the sea yet more wrathful.
Those tired with toil thought they were lost.
Each called on the deity they thought would deliver,
Some to a giant that honoured honest oaths, 165
Diana the maiden or dangerous Neptune,
Mohammed or Margot, the moon, or the sun,
Each prayed to the power on which they'd pinned their hopes.
Then the pluckiest sailor spoke, close to despair,
"We're lodging here some loser; an outlaw perhaps, 170
Who has angered his god and got himself on board.
We're all sinking in his sin, suffering for his sake.
I advise we deal out straws—each one of us draws,
Whoever gets the shortest gets shipped overside,
When we're rid of the wretch, we can reasonably trust 175
That the storm master will have mercy on the rest of us."
All gave their assent, and assembled readily,
Flushed out from every foothold to learn their fate.
A deft-footed tiller-man trawled below deck
To seek more sailors for the sorting of straws. 180
The only fellow there he was able to find
Was Jonah the Jew, wedged in the dark.
He had fled in fear from the brawl of the flood
To the bottom of the boat and lay on a board
Huddled hard to the rudder—heaven's revenge, 185
Slobber-chopped in slumber, snores in his sleep.
The sailor scuffs him with his foot and orders him to stand:
"May the devil haul you from your dreams to hell!"
He catches him by the clasp that fastens his cloak
Hauls him up by his chest and heaves him on deck, 190
Cross-examines him curtly: "What cause do you have
To sleep so soundly through the torment we suffered?"
They sort the lots swiftly; pass them around:
Each time, it's Jonah with the shortest straw.

195	Þenne ascryed þay hym sckete and asked ful loude:
	"What þe deuel hatz þou don, doted wrech?
	What seches þou on see, synful schrewe,
	With þy lastes so luþer to lose uus uchone?
	Hatz þou, gome, no governour ne god on to calle,
200	Þat þou þus slydes on slepe when þou slayn worþes?
	Of what londe art þou lent, what laytes þou here,
	Whyder in worlde þat þou wylt, and what is þyn arnde?
	Lo, þy dom is þe dyȝt, for þy dedes ille.
	Do gyf glory to þy godde, er þou glyde hens."
205	"I am an Ebru," quoþ he, "of Israyl borne;
	Þat Wyȝe I worchyp, iwysse, þat wroȝt alle þynges,
	Alle þe worlde with þe welkyn, þe wynde and þe sternes,
	And alle þat wonez þer withinne, at a worde one.
	Alle þis meschef for me is made at þys tyme,
210	For I haf greved my God and gulty am founden;
[f86ʳ]	Forþy berez me to þe borde and baþes me þeroute,
	Er gete ȝe no happe, I hope forsoþe."
	He ossed hym by unnynges þat þay undernomen
	Þat he watz flawen fro þe face of frelych Dryȝtyn:
215	Þenne such a ferde on hem fel and flayed hem withinne
	Þat þay ruyt hym to rowwe, and letten þe rynk one.
	Haþeles hyȝed in haste with ores ful longe,
	Syn her sayl watz hem aslypped, on sydez to rowe,
	Hef and hale upon hyȝt to helpen hymselven.
220	Bot al watz nedles note: þat nolde not bityde.
	In bluber of þe blo flod bursten her ores.
	Þenne hade þay noȝt in her honde þat hem help myȝt;
	Þenne nas no coumfort to kever, ne counsel non oþer,
	Bot Jonas into his juis jugge bylyve.
225	Fryst þay prayen to þe Prynce þat prophetes serven
	Þat He gef hem þe grace to greven Hym never,
	Þat þay in balelez blod þer blenden her handez,
	Þaȝ þat haþel wer His þat þay here quelled.
	Tyd by top and bi to þay token hym synne;
230	Into þat lodlych loȝe þay luche hym sone.
	He watz no tytter outtulde þat tempest ne sessed:
	Þe se saȝtled þerwith as sone as ho moȝt.
	Þenne þaȝ her takel were torne þat totered on yþes,
	Styffe stremes and streȝt hem strayned a whyle,
235	Þat drof hem dryȝlych adoun þe depe to serve,

---

211. baþes] MS baþeþes

They accost him aggressively, demand that he answer them: 195
"What the devil have you done, you doddering wretch?
What seek you from the sea, you sinful scum,
With your treacherous tricks to destroy us all?
Don't you have a god or a guv'nor you can gob to,
Than crash out cowardly when you're set to be killed? 200
Where's your homeland? What do you look for here?
Where are you headed? What errand are you on?
What you've done's been noticed. Your number's up!
Best get praying, pal, before you walk the plank."
"I am a Hebrew," said Jonah, "born in Israel, 205
The power that I praise made all that exists:
The world and the skies; the winds and the stars,
And all who live therein—with a single word.
I am responsible for the recent wrath,
I have angered my God and been found guilty: 210
So, haul me to the edge and hurl me overboard,
Otherwise I believe all luck will be lost."
He gestured through signs so they could see
He had fled from the face of his gracious Lord.
Then panic gripped them, and pinched their guts, 215
They race to get rowing to leave the wretch on his own.
The men hurried busily with full-blooded blades
To row from the sides since their sail was spent.
They heaved and hauled hoping to save themselves,
But their efforts were futile for all of their fuss, 220
The boiling black flood broke up their oars,
They're left empty handed; nothing to help them,
Hard work, heartening words, all worthless,
Save Jonah's judge bring judgement at once.
First, they pray to the Prince whom the prophets serve 225
That he grant them grace, should they aggrieve him,
(Bathing their hands in un-battled blood),
If the man they murder here was his mate.
That said, they seize Jonah swiftly by his hair
And throw him in the tumult of the tempest at once. 230
No sooner dispatched, the storm-waves cease,
And the sea settles down as soon as it could.
But the mariners' tackle was torn to bits,
Strong currents caught them and kept them spinning,
Plunged them persistently to the care of the depths 235

Tyl a swetter ful swyþe hem sweʒed to bonk.
Þer watz lovyng on lofte, when þay þe londe wonnen,
To oure mercyable God, on Moyses wyse,
With sacrafyse upset, and solempne vowes,
240 And graunted Hym on to be God and graythly non oþer.
Þaʒ þay be jolef for joye, Jonas ʒet dredes;
Þaʒ he nolde suffer no sore, his seele is on anter;
For whatso worþed of þat wyʒe fro he in water dipped,
Hit were a wonder to wene, ʒif holy wryt nere.
245 Now is Jonas þe Jwe jugged to drowne;
Of þat schended schyp men schowved hym sone.
[f86ᵛ] A wylde walterande whal, as Wyrde þen schaped,
Þat watz beten fro þe abyme, bi þat bot flotte,
And watz war of þat wyʒe þat þe water soʒte,
250 And swyftely swenged hym to swepe, and his swolʒ opened;
Þe folk ʒet haldande his fete, þe fysch hym tyd hentes;
Withouten towche of any tothe he tult in his þrote.
Thenne he swengez and swayves to þe se boþem,
Bi mony rokkez ful roʒe and rydelande strondes,
255 Wyth þe mon in his mawe malskred in drede,
As lyttel wonder hit watz, ʒif he wo dreʒed,
For nade þe hyʒe Heven-Kyng, þurʒ His honde myʒt,
Warded þis wrech man in warlowes guttez,
What lede moʒt leve bi lawe of any kynde,
260 Þat any lyf myʒt be lent so longe hym withinne?
Bot he watz sokored by þat Syre þat syttes so hiʒe,
Þaʒ were wanlez of wele in wombe of þat fissche,
And also dryven þurʒ þe depe and in derk walterez.
Lorde, colde watz his cumfort, and his care huge,
265 For he knew uche a cace and kark þat hym lymped,
How fro þe bot into þe blober watz with a best lachched,
And þrwe in at hit þrote withouten þret more,
As mote in at a munster dor, so mukel wern his chawlez.
He glydes in by þe giles þurʒ glaym ande glette,
270 Relande in by a rop, a rode þat hym þoʒt,
Ay hele over hed hourlande aboute,
Til he blunt in a blok as brod as a halle;
And þer he festnes þe fete and fathmez aboute,

---

240. on] MS vn
245. to] MS to to
259. leve] MS lyue

Until a waft of wind winnowed them to safety.
When they struck solid sand, they praised to the skies
Our merciful Maker, as Moses once did.
They made sacrifice and solemnly swore their allegiance
To the one true God, threw over the others.   240
While they're jubilant with joy, Jonah's got the jip.
Dodging discomfort, he's dunked in more danger.
You'd hardly believe what happened to him then,
Were it not for the truth of the biblical tale.
Now Jonah the Jew is doomed to drown,   245
Tossed without ceremony from the storm-torn ship.
God forced a fierce, floundering fish
To be flung from the sea floor to the floating boat.
The whale was aware of the wretch in the waters,
Swiftly surged to snatch him, jaws open wide.   250
Downs him in one, still dangling from the sailors' hands,
Velvets his teeth so he tumbles down his throat.
Then the whale sweeps imperiously to the bed of the sea
By treacherous rocks and wrestling sands
With a man in his maw mesmerised with fear.   255
Small wonder that he was wracked with worry
For if the High King of Heaven with the might of his hands
Had not guarded Jonah in the giant's guts,
Who could believe by any law of logic
That he could long survive, so long inside?   260
And yet the Lord aloft lessens his distress,
Though he abandoned all hope in his dismal abyss
With the assault of the ocean and its starkest waves.
Cold crumbs of comfort in a crisis so bleak,
He was in no doubt at all of his dangerous plight,   265
Cast from the boat, he'd been caught by a beast,
Gobbled in its gorge with no greater force
Than a dust-speck sailing through the door of a church   268a
(So enormous and huge were the whale's open jaws).   268b
He slides in through its gills, slobbered with slime,
Reeled in by a rope on what seemed a road,   270
Hurled ever forwards, head over heels,
Until he finally fetched up in what seemed a fine hall.
He finds his feet, gapes around baffled

And stod vp in his stomak þat stank as þe devel.
275 Þer in saym and in sorȝe þat savoured as helle,
Þer watz bylded his bour þat wyl no bale suffer.
And þenne he lurkkes and laytes where watz le best,
In uche a nok of his navel, bot nowhere he fyndez
No rest ne recoverer, bot ramel ande myre,
280 In wych gut so ever he gotz, bot ever is God swete;
And þer he lenged at þe last, and to þe Lede called:
"Now, Prynce, of Þy prophete pite Þou have.
[f87ʳ] Þaȝ I be fol and fykel and falce of my hert,
Dewoyde now Þy vengaunce, þurȝ vertu of rauthe;
285 Thaȝ I be gulty of gyle, as gaule of prophetes,
Þou art God, and alle gowdez ar grayþely Þyn owen.
Haf now mercy of Þy man and his mysdedes,
And preve Þe lyȝtly a Lorde in londe and in water."
With þat he hitte to a hyrne and helde hym þerinne,
290 Þer no defoule of no fylþe watz fest hym abute;
Þer he sete also sounde, saf for merk one,
As in þe bulk of þe bote þer he byfore sleped.
So in a bouel of þat best he bidez on lyve,
Þre dayes and þre nyȝt, ay þenkande on Dryȝtyn,
295 His myȝt and His merci, His mesure þenne.
Now he knawez Hym in care þat couþe not in sele.
Ande ever walteres þis whal bi wyldren depe,
Þurȝ mony a regioun ful roȝe, þurȝ ronk of his wylle;
For þat mote in his mawe mad hym, I trowe,
300 Þaȝ hit lyttel were hym wyth, to wamel at his hert;
Ande as sayled þe segge, ay sykerly he herde
Þe bygge borne on his bak and bete on his sydes.
þen a prayer ful prest þe prophete þer maked;
On þis wyse, as I wene (his wordez were mony):
305 "Lorde, to Þe haf I cleped in carez ful stronge;
Out of þe hole Þou me herde of hellen wombe;
I calde, and Þou knew myn uncler steven.
Þou diptez me of þe depe se into þe dymme hert,
Þe grete flem of Þy flod folded me umbe;
310 Alle þe gotez of Þy guferes and groundelez powlez,
And Þy stryvande stremez of stryndez so many,
In on daschande dam dryvez me over.

---

294. þre nyȝt] MS þe nyȝt

And stands up in the stomach that stank like a cess pit,
In sludge and shit that smelt like Hell.   275
Some bedroom for the bloke who'd bailed out!
He peers and pokes for a palette to rest on,
In every twist of intestine but finds nothing,
No cushion for his blows, just cack and bolus,
In whichever gut he goes. God's always so gracious!   280
All hope lost he calls to his Lord:
"Now, Prince, have pity on your prophet.
Though I'm dim, deceitful, and dishonest,
Swerve from your vengeance through the virtue of ruth,
Though I'm guilty of guile, galled to be a prophet,   285
You are God, and all goodness belongs only to you.
Have mercy on your man and his criminal acts,
Prove yourself promptly an omnipotent Prince."
Then he scuttles to a corner and keeps himself close,
Almost no ordure anywhere near him.   290
He sits there safe, save that it's dark,
Like the bottom of the boat where he slumbered before.
So in the bowels of that beast he bides his time,
Three days and three nights, thinking on God:
His might, His mercy and His measure,   295
When happy, he was ignorant, now harassed, he knows Him.
Still the whale wallows through the depths of the wild,
Ploughs proudly through places perilously rough.
Though that shrimp in his paunch was pesky—I'm sure,
It was too puny a pest to make him puke.   300
As they sailed on the sea, the man constantly heard
The beat of the sea on the beast's back and ribs.
The prophet was panicked and prayed to God—
It was a jumble of jargon, but here's the gist:
"Lord, I have called to you, carked with thole,   305
You heard me, from the hole of the pit of hell.
I called and you caught my quavering voice,
You dipped me deeply in the dark sea's heart,
Its furious flow was fast all around me,
The bulging brine and bottomless depths,   310
Wrangling waters, waves at war,
Drenched me with the deluge of a broken dam,

And ȝet I sayde as I seet in þe se boþem:
'Careful am I, kest out fro Þy cler yȝen
And desevered fro Þy syȝt; ȝet surely I hope
Efte to trede on Þy temple and teme to Þyselven.'
I am wrapped in water to my wo stoundez;
Þe abyme byndes þe body þat I byde inne;
Þe pure poplande hourle playes on my heved;
To laste mere of uche a mount, Man, am I fallen;
Þe barrez of uche a bonk ful bigly me haldes,
Þat I may lachche no lont, and Þou my lyf weldes.
Þou schal releve me, Renk, whil Þy ryȝt slepez,
Þurȝ myȝt of Þy mercy þat mukel is to tryste.
For when þ'acces of anguych watz hid in my sawle,
Þenne I remembred me ryȝt of my rych Lorde,
Prayande Him for peté His prophete to here,
Þat into His holy hous myn orisoun moȝt entre.
I haf meled with Þy maystres mony longe day,
Bot now I wot wyterly þat þose unwyse ledes
Þat affyen hym in vanyté and in vayne þynges
For þink þat mountes to noȝt her mercy forsaken;
Bot I dewoutly awowe, þat verray betz halden,
Soberly to do Þe sacrafyse when I schal save worþe,
And offer Þe for my hele a ful hol gyfte,
And halde goud þat Þou me hetes: haf here my trauthe."
Thenne oure Fader to þe fysch ferslych biddez
Þat he hym sput spakly upon spare drye.
Þe whal wendez at His wylle and a warþe fyndez,
And þer he brakez up þe buyrne as bede hym oure Lorde.
Þenne he swepe to þe sonde in sluchched cloþes:
Hit may wel be þat mester were his mantyle to wasche.
Þe bonk þat he blosched to and bode hym bisyde
Wern of þe regiounes ryȝt þat he renayed hade.
Þenne a wynde of Goddez worde efte þe wyȝe bruxlez:
"Nylt þou never to Nunive bi no kynnez wayez?"
"Ȝisse, Lorde," quoþ þe lede, "lene me Þy grace
For to go at Þi gre: me gaynez non oþer."
"Ris, aproche þen to prech, lo, þe place here.
Lo, My lore is in þe loke, lauce hit þerinne."
Þenne þe renk radly ros as he myȝt,

---

313. sayde] MS say
348. non] MS mon

And still I said, from bottom of the sea:
'I am desolate, dashed from your undimmed eyes,
Struck from your sight, but I sorely hope   315
I may yet enter your house and be at one with you.'
I'm assailed by the sea, my soul is stoned,
My living flesh held fast in flood,
The heaving surge hammers my head,
At the final hurdle of each hill I fall—   320
The steep stone banks stop my attempts
To alight on dry land while you rule my life.
You must mind me (a man), while your majesty sleeps,
Through the reach of your ruth on which I rely,
For when unbearable anguish battered my soul   325
I remembered right away my gracious Ruler,
Prayed Him to hear His prophet out of pity,
That my orison might enter His holy house.
I've whiled away my days, wording your elders,
But I know now for a fact that foolish folk,   330
Who trust in vanity and trivial things,
Blow their hope of bliss for worthless bling.
But solemnly I swear to be true to my speech,
When I'm saved, I'll serve you with sacrifice,
And offer you for my health, a wholesome gift,   335
I'll obey your orders: you have my word on it."
So our Father, fiercely, commands the great fish
To puke the prophet pronto onto dry land.
Wending to his will, the whale finds a wharf
And barfs up the prophet as his superior bid.   340
Jonah swims to the sand in stench-stained clothes,
He could use some clean water to wash his cloak!
The shores that he saw and those where he rested
Were the very same ones he vowed he wouldn't visit.
But then a blast of God's breath berates the man: 345
"No way you're going to Nineveh, then, eh?"
"Of course I'll go Lord," he said, "grant me your grace
To do what you bid me—besides, I've no choice."
"Then prepare to preach, the place is close by,
My laws are lost there, make them listen up!"   350
Best foot forward, the prophet moves fast,

And to Ninive þat naȝt he neȝed ful even;
Hit watz a cete ful syde and selly of brede;
On to þrenge þerþurȝe watz þre dayes dede.
Þat on journay ful joynt Jonas hym ȝede, 355
Er ever he warpped any worde to wyȝe þat he mette,
And þenne he cryed so cler þat kenne myȝt alle
Þe trwe tenor of his teme; he tolde on þis wyse:
"Ȝet schal forty dayez fully fare to an ende,
And þenne schal Ninive be nomen and to noȝt worþe; 360
Truly þis ilk toun schal tylte to grounde;
Up-so-doun schal ȝe dumpe depe to þe abyme,
To be swolȝed swyftly wyth þe swart erþe,
And alle þat lyvyes hereinne lose þe swete."
Þis speche sprang in þat space and spradde alle aboute, 365
To borges and to bacheleres þat in þat burȝ lenged;
Such a hidor hem hent and a hatel drede,
Þat al chaunged her chere and chylled at þe hert.
Þe segge sesed not ȝet, bot sayde ever ilyche:
"Þe verray vengaunce of God schal voyde þis place!" 370
Þenne þe peple pitosly pleyned ful stylle,
And for þe drede of Dryȝtyn doured in hert;
Heter hayrez þay hent þat asperly bited,
And þose þay bounden to her bak and to her bare sydez,
Dropped dust on her hede, and dymly bisoȝten 375
Þat þat penaunce plesed Him þat playnez on her wronge.
And ay he cryes in þat kyth tyl þe kyng herde,
And he radly upros and ran fro his chayer,
His ryche robe he torof of his rigge naked,
And of a hep of askes he hitte in þe myddez. 380
He askez heterly a hayre and hasped hym umbe,
Sewed a sekke þerabof, and syked ful colde;
Þer he dased in þat duste, with droppande teres,
Wepande ful wonderly alle his wrange dedes.
Þenne sayde he to his serjauntes: "Samnes yow bilyve; 385
Do dryve out a decre, demed of myselven,
Þat alle þe bodyes þat ben withinne þis borȝ quyk,
Boþe burnes and bestes, burdez and childer,
Uch prynce, uche prest, and prelates alle,
Alle faste frely for her falce werkes; 390
Sesez childer of her sok, soghe hem so never,
Ne best bite on no brom, ne no bent nauþer,

Sets out tout de suite that very same night.
The city of Nineveh sprawled in all directions,
To trek through it all would take three days.
Jonah kept on track, never took a stop, 355
Preached without pause to each person he met
In no uncertain terms, so all did know
What his words truly meant. He told them,
"Before forty days have come to their finish,
Nineveh will be captured, crushed into nothing, 360
Truly, this town shall tumble to the ground,
You'll be dumped in the pit, upside down,
Promptly swallowed by pitch-black silt,
All those who live here will lose their lives."
The speech spread like wildfire throughout the city, 365
To all its residents, whatever their rank.
Such horror harrowed them and acrid dread,
Their cheeks turned to chalk; their hearts chilled.
But the teacher didn't cease from telling his tale,
"The great vengeance of God shall gut this place." 370
The people wept piteously, wailed at length,
Aghast at God's might, they grieved in their hearts,
Grabbed rough hair shirts that savagely scratched,
Bound them on their backs and on their bare skin,
Scattered ashes on their heads and gloomily sought 375
To appease with penance God's ire for their sins.
The crisis in the city became known to the king,
He rose from his throne, and rushed out at once,
Rips the rich robe from off his bare back,
Hurls it in the heart of a heap of ashes. 380
He demands a hair shirt and dons it immediately,
Sews some sackcloth to it, sighing, distraught.
He's stunned in dust, tears drip from his eyes,
Crying and keening for all of his crimes.
Then he summoned his officers: "Assemble at once, 385
Proclaim this decree that I have composed:
Any living thing that lives within my law,
All men, women, children, and animals,
Every prince, every priest, every person
Shall fast without stint for their sinful deeds. 390
Cease to suckle children; even if they sicken,
Let no beast graze on grass, or even on gorse,

Passe to no pasture, ne pike non erbes,
Ne non oxe to no hay, ne no horse to water.
395 Al schal crye, forclemmed, with alle oure clere strenþe;
Þe rurd schal ryse to Hym þat rawþe schal have;
What wote oþer wyte may ȝif þe Wyȝe lykes,
Þat is hende in þe hyȝt of His gentryse?
I wot His myȝt is so much, þaȝ He be myssepayed,
400 Þat in His mylde amesyng He mercy may fynde.
And if we leven þe layk of oure layth synnes,
And stylle steppen in þe styȝe He styȝtlez Hymselven,
He wyl wende of His wodschip and His wrath leve,
And forgif uus þis gult, ȝif we Hym God leven."
405 Þenne al leved on His lawe and laften her synnes,
Parformed alle þe penaunce þat þe prynce radde;
And God þurȝ His godnesse forgef as He sayde;
Þaȝ He oþer bihyȝt, withhelde His vengaunce.
Muche sorȝe þenne satteled upon segge Jonas;
410 He wex as wroth as þe wynde towarde oure Lorde.
So hatz anger onhit his hert, he callez
A prayer to þe hyȝe Prynce, for pyne, on þys wyse:
"I biseche Þe, Syre, now Þou self jugge;
Watz not þis ilk my worde þat worþen is nouþe,
415 Þat I kest in my cuntre, when Þou Þy carp sendez
Þat I schulde tee to þys toun Þi talent to preche?
Wel knew I Þi cortaysye, Þy quoynt soffraunce,
Þy bounte of debonerte and Þy bene grace,
Þy longe abydyng wyth lur, Þy late vengaunce;
420 And ay Þy mercy is mete, be mysse never so huge.
I wyst wel, when I hade worded quatsoever I cowþe
To manace alle þise mody men þat in þis mote dowellez,
Wyth a prayer and a pyne þay myȝt her pese gete,
And þerfore I wolde haf flowen fer into Tarce.
425 Now, Lorde, lach out my lyf, hit lastes to longe.
Bed me bilyve my bale-stour and bryng me on ende,
[f89ʳ] For me were swetter to swelt as swyþe, as me þynk,
Þen lede lenger Þi lore þat þus me les makez."
Þe soun of oure Soverayn þen swey in his ere,
430 Þat upbraydes þis burne upon a breme wyse:
"Herk, renk, is þis ryȝt so ronkly to wrath

---

411. he] MS ye

They're prohibited pasture or to nibble on plants,
No hay for the ox; no water for the horse.
Famished and faint, we'll wail with full strength, 395
Our clamour will cry to our Maker for mercy.
Who can be sure though, it'll meet with His pleasure,
Generous though He be, great with graciousness?
His might's so immense, even if He's storming,
His gentle mildness may make Him merciful 400
If we abandon our abandonment to abhorrent sins.
If we stick to the track that He taught us Himself,
His choler will cool; He'll cast off his wrath,
God will forgive our guilt if we believe in Him."
They believed the Lord's law; left sin behind, 405
And performed the penance that the king prescribed.
Out of his goodness, God gave them forgiveness.
He'd decreed differently but dispensed with his wrath.
The red mist of dissent then descends upon Jonah,
He was livid with his Lord, and lets rip, 410
Rabid with rage, he gives God both barrels,
Hurt, he addresses his Highness, thus:
"I urge you, judge, to judge yourself,
Isn't this exactly what I said would happen
When sat at home, I answered your summons, 415
To travel to this town to tell your intent?
I'd sussed your courtesy, your exquisite sufferance,
Your bounteous beneficence, and your benevolence,
Your stalwart forbearance, your slow vengeance,
Your measured mercy, however huge the crime. 420
I knew only too well when I'd worked out my words
To threaten the thugs that live in this town,
They might be pardoned for their penance and prayers—
That's why I wanted to whizz off to Tarshish.
Now, Lord, take my life; it's lasted too long, 425
Sentence me swiftly and end my agony.
I'd much rather die, reach my time right here,
Than keep peddling your piffle that paints me a liar."
The voice of our Sovereign vroomed in his ear,
Refuting in fury the fool's rash speech. 430
"Listen up, wretch, you've no right to lecture me

For any dede þat I haf don oþer demed þe ȝet?"
Jonas al joyles and janglande upryses,
And haldez out on est half of þe hyȝe place,
435 And farandely on a felde he fettelez hym to bide,
For to wayte on þat won what schulde worþe after.
Þer he busked hym a bour, þe best þat he myȝt,
Of hay and of ever-ferne and erbez a fewe,
For hit watz playn in þat place for plyande grevez,
440 For to schylde fro þe schene oþer any schade keste.
He bowed under his lyttel boþe, his bak to þe sunne,
And þer he swowed and slept sadly al nyȝt,
Þe whyle God of His grace ded growe of þat soyle
Þe fayrest bynde hym abof þat ever burne wyste.
445 When þe dawande day Dryȝtyn con sende,
Þenne wakened þe wyȝ under wodbynde,
Loked alofte on þe lef þat lylled grene;
Such a lefsel of lof never lede hade,
For hit watz brod at þe boþem, boȝted on lofte,
450 Happed upon ayþer half, a hous as hit were,
A nos on þe norþ syde and nowhere non ellez,
Bot al schet in a schaȝe þat schaded ful cole.
Þe gome glyȝt on þe grene graciouse leves,
Þat ever wayved a wynde so wyþe and so cole;
455 Þe schyre sunne hit umbeschon, þaȝ no schafte myȝt
Þe mountaunce of a lyttel mote upon þat man schyne.
Þenne watz þe gome so glad of his gay logge,
Lys loltrande þerinne lokande to toune;
So blyþe of his wodbynde he balteres þerunder,
460 Þat of no diete þat day þe devel haf he roȝt.
And ever he laȝed as he loked þe loge alle aboute,
And wysched hit were in his kyth þer he wony schulde,
[f89ᵛ] On heȝe upon Effraym oþer Ermonnes hillez:
"Iwysse, a worþloker won to welde I never keped."
465 And quen hit neȝed to naȝt nappe hym bihoved;
He slydez on a sloumbe-slep sloghe under leves,
Whil God wayned a worme þat wrot upe þe rote,
And wyddered watz þe wodbynde bi þat þe wyȝe wakned;
And syþen He warnez þe west to waken ful softe,
470 And sayez unte Zeferus þat he syfle warme,
Þat þer quikken no cloude bifore þe cler sunne,

---

459. þerunder] MS þervnde

For anything I've done or dealt to you yet."
Jonah gets up, gurning in a grump,
And strides to the easternmost side of the city.
He finds a fine field and settles himself down   435
To wait until he learns the lie of the land.
He builds himself a boudoir, the best that he was able,
From the fag-ends of foliage he could forage—
For the place was parched, no Aeolian coppice
To shield him from scorch or to cast cool shade.   440
He crawled into his tiny booth with his back to the sun,
Sank into sleep and slumbered soundly through the night.
(Meanwhile God, from His grace, grew from the soil
The bonniest bine above him that ever was known.)
When God made the dawn deliver the day   445
Jonah awoke with a woodbine above him,
And glanced up at green leaves, that fluttered serene.
No-one had ever owned such a beautiful bower,
For it was broad at its base and vaulted above,
Enclosed all around, as though it were a house.   450
The only opening was in the aspect to the north,
But set within a spinney that lent full shade.
He looks up at the ceiling of the soft green leaves
That wafted softly in the balm-borne breeze.
The bright sun beat down but not one of its beams,   455
Not a glimmer of glint, glances that man.
Then Jonah rejoices in his jolly new lodge,
He lolls at his leisure, looks back to town,
So delighted with his woodbine, he dances underneath—
The devil can devour his dinner today!   460
He can't stop laughing as he looks where he's stopped,
And hankers for the same, when he's safe back home,
High up on Ephraim or the Hermon Hills.
A cosier home he could never hope to own.
And when nightfall came and he needed to nap,   465
He slid into sleep, slumbered under leaves.
(Meanwhile God made a maggot to munch up the root,
And by the time the man awoke, his woodbine had withered.)
Then He tells the West Wind to awaken softly
And bids Zephyrus to blow with blistering force   470
So no clouds cluster to scarf the sun's glare.

And ho schal busch up ful brode and brenne as a candel.
Þen wakened þe wyȝe of his wyl dremes,
And blusched to his wodbynde þat broþely watz marred,
475 Al welwed and wasted þo worþelych leves;
Þe schyre sunne hade hem schent er ever þe schalk wyst.
And þen hef up þe hete and heterly brenned;
Þe warm wynde of þe weste, wertes he swyþez.
Þe man marred on þe molde þat moȝt hym not hyde
480 His wodbynde watz away, he weped for sorȝe;
With hatel anger and hot, heterly he callez:
"A, Þou Maker of man, what maystery Þe þynkez
Þus Þy freke to forfare forbi alle oþer?
With alle meschef þat Þou may, never Þou me sparez;
485 I kevered me a cumfort þat now is caȝt fro me,
My wodbynde so wlonk þat wered my heved.
Bot now I se Þou art sette my solace to reve;
Why ne dyȝttez Þou me to diȝe? I dure to longe."
Ȝet oure Lorde to þe lede laused a speche:
490 "Is þis ryȝtwys, þou renk, alle þy ronk noyse,
So wroth for a wodbynde to wax so sone?
Why art þou so waymot, wyȝe, for so lyttel?"
"Hit is not lyttel," quoþ þe lede, "bot lykker to ryȝt;
I wolde I were of þis worlde wrapped in moldez."
495 "Þenne byþenk þe, mon, if þe forþynk sore,
If I wolde help My hondewerk, haf þou no wonder;
Þou art waxen so wroth for þy wodbynde,
And travayledez never to tent hit þe tyme of an howre,
[f90ʳ] Bot at a wap hit here wax and away at anoþer,
500 And ȝet lykez þe so luþer, þi lyf woldez þou tyne.
Þenne wyte not Me for þe werk, þat I hit wolde help,
And rwe on þo redles þat remen for synne;
Fyrst I made hem Myself of materes Myn one,
And syþen I loked hem ful longe and hem on lode hade.
505 And if I My travayl schulde tyne of termes so longe,
And type doun ȝonder toun when hit turned were,
Þe sor of such a swete place burde synk to My hert,
So mony malicious mon as mournez þerinne.
And of þat soumme ȝet arn summe, such sottez formadde,
510 As lyttel barnez on barme þat never bale wroȝt,
And wymmen unwytté þat wale ne couþe

Bare faced, she'll rise, and blaze like a torch.
Then Jonah rouses from his restless dreams
And sees that his woodbine is savagely burnt,
The once lush leaves all shrivelled and shrunk, 475
The sun had fried them before the prophet knew,
Then turned up the heat to burn even brighter—
The warm west wind withered all that grew.
With his cover blown, he curls up and blubs
For his vanished green gourd. He weeps in anguish, 480
Sizzling with spleen, he shouts out irascibly,
"Lord of Creation, what kind of conquest is it
To assault your servant, single me out,
With all the mayhem you can muster, molest me endlessly?
I'd just got settled, now all of that's scotched, 485
My impressive canopy that kept me alive,
Now I see you are set on destroying my rest—
Just judge me to die. I'm too jiggered to live!"
Despite the man's insolence, God answers him:
"Is it reasonable, wretch, to rant with such ignorance, 490
And to get so angry because your gourd is no more,
Why do you peeve, man, over something so petty?"
"It's not petty," said the man, "it's a matter of principle.
I want the earth to yawn open and swallow me up."
"Think about this then, if you think you're bereft, 495
Why wouldn't I care for what I've created?
You've thrown such a tantrum for your precious tree,
Which you never thought to nurture at any point
(Here one minute and away the next),
You're so dismayed, you're determined to die. 500
Don't reprimand Me, man, for minding what I made,
And saving errant souls who repent their sins,
First, I made them Myself from My own elements,
Then fostered them long, and found for them always,
And if My labours were lost after such long love, 505
That town was torn down though they'd become contrite,
The sorrow of the sweet place would pierce My heart—
There, even now, once-wicked folk weep.
Amongst them are many, so ill in their minds,
They can't fathom the difference of down and across, 510
Or reason how you reckon the right from the left,

>   Þat on hande fro at oþer, for alle þis hyȝe worlde.
>   Bitwene þe stele and þe stayre disserne noȝt cunen,
>   What rule renes in roun bitwene þe ryȝt hande
> 515 And his lyfte, þaȝ his lyf schulde lost be þerfor;
>   And als þer ben doumbe bestez in þe burȝ mony,
>   Þat may not synne in no syt hemselven to greve.
>   Why schulde I wrath wyth hem, syþen wyȝez wyl torne,
>   And cum and cnawe Me for Kyng and My carpe leve?
> 520 Wer I as hastif as þou heere, were harme lumpen;
>   Couþe I not þole bot as þou, þer þryved ful fewe,
>   I may not be so malicious and mylde be halden,
>   For malyse is noȝt to mayntyne boute mercy withinne.
>   Be noȝt so gryndel, godman, bot go forth þy wayes;
> 525 Be preve and be pacient in payne and in joye;
>   For he þat is to rakel to renden his cloþez
>   Mot efte sitte with more unsounde to sewe hem togeder."
>   Forþy when poverté me enprecez and paynez innoȝe
>   Ful softly with suffraunce saȝttel me bihovez;
> 530 Forþy penaunce and payne topreve hit in syȝt
>   Þat pacience is a nobel poynt, þaȝ hit displese ofte.

Amen.

---

512. for] MS fol
520. as þou] MS a þou
522. malicious] MS malcious
523. noȝt] MS noȝ
524. noȝt] MS noȝ

Even if the consequences cost them their lives:
Like babes at the breast, that brew no bale,
Women at their wits' end, too overwrought
To say which hand is which, whatever the cost, 515
And the dozens of dumb beasts who bide in the town,
Who lack the capacity to sin or to sorrow.
Why should I try those who return to Me,
Acknowledge Me King and keep to My teaching?
Were I as rash as you are, all would be wrecked, 520
Could I thole only like you do, there'd be few left alive.
I can't be held merciful yet act with malice,
The power to maim must be tempered with mercy.
Quit grizzling and growling, and get yourself going,
Be steadfast and stoic in sorrow or in joy; 525
Those who are quick to cut up their clothes
Will sit with worse scraps to stitch them back up."
So, if I'm skint, or in a scrape, or I've hit the skids,
I must weather the storm—and with serenity.
The stiff upper lip is the ultimate proof 530
That patience is a pip that's properly unpleasant.

                      Amen

Notes on the Text and Translation

1] The first and last lines are especially challenging to translate because of the various senses of "poynt." **MED: pointe (n) 1. (a)** A small dot marked on a surface; also, a punctuation mark, period; (b) a small hole; prick, puncture; (c) a spot of dirt; **2.** A small amount, the smallest part; the least bit; **3.** (a) A point in space, a place, spot, location; (b) the centre point; fig. that upon which all depends, or about which all revolves; **4.** (a) A brief period of time, an instant, a moment; (b) a point in time; **5.** (a) A critical or decisive moment or situation, ... (c) an opportune moment, opportunity, a chance; **6.** (a) A subject, topic, theme; question for discussion, issue; also, a question; (b) the essential part of a subject; the central theme; (c) an authoritative teaching, principle, proposition; (d) object, end, goal; also, purpose; **7.** (a) a stage in a progression; an article of faith; (b) a rule, regulation; ... **9.** (a) An activity, action, operation; **10.** (a) State of being, condition, situation, disposition; (b) good condition; (c) a good quality, virtue; (d) a characteristic, trait; reputation; **11.** (a) The sharp-pointed end of a sword, knife, needle, staff; **12.** (c) one of the angular points of a figure or star. My choice of "pip" captures the senses of tininess, illness, pain, and frustration concerning the seeds of a fruit, which, though bitter, are necessary for renewed growth. A pip is also a sign of military achievement, the recognition of good qualities in service; a sign of rank; and in sound, an acoustic moment in a sequence (**OED pip (n). 3**). See also note to line 531.

2] **hassel backed** Obviously, the poet would not have encountered potatoes, slashed or otherwise. The recipe for Hasselback potatoes was first introduced in a restaurant named Hasselbacken in Stockholm, Sweden, in the 1940s. My use of this punning image suggests the heaviness of hearts that are burdened with hurt. (A potato looks like a biological heart in shape.)

3] **broil** translates "swelme" [heat] with its pun on "quarrel." I have reorganized the order of the line and introduced the interpersonal *you*.

6] **thran** A Northern Irish word for "stubborn, awkward." **thole** The Old English verb for "to suffer" is still used in some dialectal varieties of Modern English.

9] **Holy Day** is a Sunday or a feast day for a saint or other important event in the Christian liturgy. A **High Mass** is a solemn celebration of the Christian service of the Eucharist.

10] **Matthew** The disciple of Jesus who wrote the first Gospel of the New Testament. The lines that follow are a version of the Beatitudes from Christ's Sermon on the Mount, Matthew 5:1–12. This was the Gospel reading appointed for the Feast of All Saints to commemorate those who had died.

11] **outcomes** While "happes" is translated as "blessing" in the following lines to match the poet's "happen" to translate the Vulgate's "Beati," "outcomes" is much closer to the Middle English sense of "hap" as something which simply occurs; see *MED* **hap n. 2. (a).**

12] **to each** translates the two phrases which mean "diversely": "Sunderlupes" and "in a ser wyse." For discussion of this crucial line, see pp. 24–25.

14] **keys ... for keeps** literally "to hold for ever."

15] **abide** in its twin dialect senses of "live" and "endure" translates "haunte": *MED* **haunten v. (1) 2. (a)** To dwell in, live in; **5. (b)** to practice a virtue.

19] **thirst** translates "hungeres" to secure alliteration.

22] **wide open-armed** literally "in all manners."

23] **pearls polished** added in translation to chime with the representation of purity in *Pearl*.

25] **curb their rancour** literally "hold their peace." The substitution secures alliteration and echoes lines 1–9.

26] **children in charity** literally "sons" and "godly."

27] **with reason** added in translation.

30] **the blameless lives** literally "in imitation of their virtues."

33] **keep a place warm** literally "put in after them."

35] **saddled with** literally "reduced to a condition called."

36] **make Patience my mistress** literally "equip myself with Patience."

37] **"P"s are two peas in a pod** literally "laid out as a team."

38] **a package, a pair you can't part** literally "are of one nature."

41] **pokes her nose in** literally "presents herself."

44] **make your life a misery** literally "he has to suffer." **however much you moan** literally "despite your mouth."

47] **tolerate** literally "like it."

52] **Rome** was the seat of the Papacy, though when the poem was written there had been a schism in the Church and there was also a Pope at Avignon in France.

54–56] These lines are knotted in syntax and meaning and require considerable expansion in prose. I have tried to retain some poetic expression while attending to the overall sense. Literally "It would be much if He didn't make me, despite my objections, and then must I suffer compulsion and ingratitude as my reward who should have bowed to his bidding according to the terms of my hire." **chunter** (54) is an informal British word that means "to mutter or grumble monotonously."

57] **lived in** added in translation. **Judea** is the name of a large territory in southern Israel. See maps of the Old and New Testaments, Appendix E.

58] **Who fell flat on his face as he tried to play safe** Literally "he attempted to stick to safety but brings misfortune upon himself."

62] **Gentiles** are peoples who are not Jews. Jonah is the only prophet in the Old Testament who preaches to Gentiles.

63–64] literally "God's noise glided to him which made him unglad, with a rough voice, breathed words into his ear." "rowned" (64) may pun on "rown" (n.) as "secret." **rattled his drum** is an attempt to catch the wordplay of the line.

65] **Stir your stumps** literally "get up."

66] **Nineveh** the capital of the Assyrian Empire. As recorded in the Old Testament, the Assyrians were enemies of the Jewish people. Nineveh is now in the Mosul region of Iraq.

68] **I'll teach you what words to say—and when to do so** literally "that in that place, at the right time, I put in your heart." "words" replaces the pronoun "that," which refers to "speeches" (67) to make the sense clearer. God will tell Jonah when to speak and what to say.

82] **hostile crowd** literally "among so many enemies." **in hock to hell** suggests the Ninevites' allegiance to the devil, literally "cursed fiends."

85] **I'll mind my back** literally "approach no nearer."

87] **Tarshish** is either the historic city of Tarsus in south-central Turkey, just inland from the Mediterranean, or the ancient city of Tartus on the Mediterranean coast of Syria. See maps in Appendix E. Jonah attempts to flee in the opposite direction to where God has commanded him to travel.

88] **likely** translates "ly3tly," which can mean "probably" or "easily."

90] **Joppa** is a port in the southern and oldest part of Tel Aviv in Israel; see maps in Appendix E. **each step a protest** literally "arguing all the time from anger."

92] **faffed to look after him** literally "indifferent about his well-being." "faffed" is an informal British word which means "considering something important a waste of time."

93] **Our Lord lounges aloof on his lofty perch** literally, "Our Lord sits," he says, "in a place so high." "lounges" is chosen to suggest complacency, "loftily" to suggest height and aloofness, and "perch" to suggest vantage point, or in British slang, a kind of voyeurism. "He says" omitted in translation; quotation marks indicate that it is Jonah who speaks.

94] **give a damn** literally "frowns not at all."

96] sharked shamefully by a crew of scum literally "torn to pieces pitifully by many scoundrels." **Sharked** dates from 1611 in the sense of tearing apart. Its current slang use means "destroyed" or "done for."

98] spies literally "finds."

100] sharpish literally "as quickly as they could."

101] dawdles on deck literally "treads on the boards."

103] windlass a winch for hauling up the sails.

104] bow-line a rope that attaches one side of a square sail to the front part of a ship. **bowsprit** a spar that projects from the prow of a ship. Its function is to extend the surface area of the front sail (**huge sheet,** line 105) as far as possible.

106] port-side the left side of the ship.

110] Tickled pink with his trick literally "so cleverly escaped."

116] Samaria a town in the middle part of Israel in the Old Testament. In the New Testament, Samaria has become a region separate from Judea; see maps in Appendix E.

119] David (c. 1035–970 BCE) was the second king of Israel. He is attributed with the authorship of 150 psalms (words written to be sung to music) that are preserved in the Book of Psalms in the Old Testament. The Psalms were at the heart of medieval Christian life and thought. Monks and nuns recited them daily; lay people spoke them in services for the Virgin Mary and for the Dead. Children learned them as the basis of teaching them their ABC. Theologians wrote extensive commentaries on the Psalms.

120] Psalter the Psalms were collected separately from the Bible in a book that came to be known as the Psalter. Wealthy lay people might own their own copy of the Psalms. The lines that follow paraphrase Psalm 93:8–9.

121] fettle your thoughts for once literally "perceive sometimes." "Fettle" is still used in some varieties of English to mean "to set in order" or "to tidy up."

126] **Convinced he's invisible, he cruises to Tarshish** literally "For he was far off in the flood on his way to Tarshish."

127] **Too slow to suss he'd been spied from the start** literally "But believe me, he was overtaken immediately."

130] **He has tricks up His sleeve** literally "He has stratagems whenever He wants."

133] **Eurus** in classical mythology is a wind from the east or southeast. **Aquilon** is the north wind.

134] "at my bidding" omitted in translation. The imperative captures that God's speech is a command.

135] **No sooner said than the summons was sped** literally "there was no time between God's speech and their action."

146] **Jonah's truculence turns treacherous trap** literally "it was a joyless plan that Jonah was in."

158] **Finery** literally "bags," which means "baggage" in the sense of "trappings"—unnecessary items.

160] **lee** shelter from the wind.

165] **giant** literally Vernagu, a giant from medieval French romance.

166] **Diana** the Roman god of chastity. **Neptune** the Roman god of the sea.

167] **Mohammed** translates "Mahoun." In Christian medieval texts, Mahoun or Mahomet was regarded as a false god. **Margot** is a heathen god found in early French romances.

188] **"May the devil haul you from your dreams to hell!"** It is not clear in whose voice this curse is uttered, though the most likely candidate is the sailor, who mutters this under his breath, and the poet records his speech indirectly. Literally, the line reads, "May Ragnel in his chains rouse him from his dreams." Ragnel is the name of a minor devil. In medieval depictions of the Judgement, sinners were often shown being dragged to hell by demons with ropes or chains; see Appendix D5. This iconography also informs line 270.

199] **guv'nor** a word from British slang that means "boss."

203] **What you've done's been noticed. Your number's up!** literally "your doom is ordained for your sinful deeds."

204] **Best get praying, pal, before you walk the plank** literally "Make sure you give glory to your God before you glide away from here."

215] **Then panic gripped them, and pinched their guts** literally "then such a fear fell on them and flayed them within."

217] **full-blooded blades** literally "with very long oars."

223] **Hard work, heartening words, all worthless** literally "there was no comfort they could obtain, nor any kind of counsel."

235] **care of the depths** literally "to serve the deep"—to be at the mercy of the deep.

236] **winnowed** literally "brought." The separation of the chaff and wheat at harvest time is often used as a metaphor for distinguishing between the saved and the damned at the Last Judgement. Throughout the depiction of the mariners' plight, the poet has selected diction which presents the episode as a mini-drama of salvation.

238] **Moses** the leader of the Israelites in their flight from Egypt, as told in the Old Testament Book of Exodus. The sacrifices made to God as thanksgiving for cleansing are narrated in the Old Testament Book of Leviticus 14:132. They became known as the law of Moses, as mentioned in the New Testament Gospel of Mark 1:44.

242–43] **Dodging discomfort, he's dunked in more danger** literally "though he didn't want to suffer any distress, his happiness is in peril." "Dunked" captures the sense of "from when he was dipped in water" at the end of line 243, which I have omitted in translation to sustain a measurable line length.

251–52] **Downs him in one, still dangling from the sailors' hands, / Velvets his teeth so he tumbles down his throat** literally "with the folk still holding his feet, the fish snatches him at once / Without any touch from his teeth he tumbles into his throat."

261] **And yet the Lord aloft lessens his distress** literally "but he was succoured by the Sire that sits on high."

262] **in his dismal abyss** literally "in the stomach of that fish."

264] **Cold crumbs of comfort in a crisis so bleak** literally "Lord! Cold was his comfort, and huge his cares."

265] **He was in no doubt at all of his dangerous plight** literally "for he knew each situation and trouble that had befallen him."

268a and 268b] I have extended line 268 over two lines but retained line numbering in tranches of five to align with the Middle English text.

272] **fine** added in translation.

276–79] **bloke who'd bailed out** literally "that will suffer no trouble." **palette** literally "shelter or castle." **cushion for his blows** literally "no rest or harbour." My diction attempts to capture the poet's juxtaposition of the filth of the whale's stomach with the trappings and spaces of an aristocratic hall.

284] **Swerve** literally "void."

288] **Prove yourself promptly an omnipotent Prince** literally "And lightly prove yourself a Lord on land and in water."

290] **Almost no ordure anywhere near him** literally "where almost no foulness of filth was around him."

299–300] **Though that shrimp in his paunch was pesky—I'm sure, / It was too puny a pest to make him puke** literally "though that mote in his maw, maddened him, I swear / It was little compared to him to make him feel sick."

303] **The prophet was panicked and prayed to God** literally "then the prophet made a prayer very quickly."

304] **It was a jumble of jargon, but here's the gist** literally "in this manner as far as I can tell, his words were many."

305] **carked with thole** literally "in very strong cares." Lines 305–36 paraphrase Psalm 68; see Appendix A3. Some medieval psalters have accompanying illustrations which depict Jonah in the sea.

307] **quavering** literally "unclear."

316] **at one with you** literally "and belong to you."

320] **At the final hurdle of each hill I fall** literally "A man, I fall at the last boundary of every mountain."

332] **bliss** literally "mercy."

345] **blast** literally "word."

348] **besides, I've no choice** literally "it doesn't profit me to do otherwise."

350] **My laws are lost there, make them listen up** literally "My lore is locked there, unloose it therein."

351] **Best foot forward, the prophet moves fast** literally "The man rose up as quickly as he could."

353] **Nineveh** has been transposed here from the previous line. **sprawled in all directions** literally "very wide and exceptionally broad."

355] **Jonah kept on track, never took a stop** literally "Jonah proceeded on his journey continuously."

366] **To all its residents, whatever their rank** literally "to burgesses and bachelors who dwelt in the town."

368] **Their cheeks turned to chalk** literally "their faces changed."

373] **hair shirts** a garment of coarse haircloth, worn next to the skin as an act of penance.

377] **crisis** literally "cry."

384] **Crying and keening for all of his crimes** literally "weeping grievously for all his misdeeds."

387] **law** literally "borough."

389] **person** literally "prelates."

392] **grass** literally "broom plants." **gorse** literally "grass or field."

397] **Who can be sure though, it'll meet with His pleasure** literally "Who knows, or may know if it pleases the Lord."

399] **even if He's storming** literally "though He be displeased."

402] **If we stick to the track that He taught us Himself** literally "and still step in the path he taught us Himself."

409] **The red mist of dissent then descends upon Jonah** literally "Huge sorrow then settled upon the man Jonah."

410] **He was livid with his Lord, and lets rip** literally "He became as angry as the wind towards our Lord."

411] **Rabid with rage, he gives God both barrels** literally "such anger has seized his heart, he calls."

412] **Hurt, he addresses his Highness, thus** literally "A prayer to the high Prince, for his suffering, in this way."

428] **piffle** literally "falsehoods."

433] **Jonah gets up, gurning in a grump** literally "Jonah was all joyless, and wrangling."

436] **To wait until he learns the lie of the land** literally "to watch what would happen in the city afterwards."

438] **From the fag-ends of foliage he could forage** literally "Of hay and of ferns, and a few grasses." **fag-ends** a word derived from the butt of a cigarette. Its more generalized sense is "the last and poorest remnants."

439] **For the place was parched, no Aeolian coppice** literally "For it was bare in that place with regard to waving groves." Aeolus was the Greek god of the wind. The adjective "Aeolian" in later poetry suggests a soft breeze that blows through trees to produce a sound like a harp.

444] **bine** is the twining stem of a plant. It is an alternative name for woodbine in recognition of the woodbine's entwining shoots.

447] **that fluttered serene** literally "that waved."

453] **He looks up at the ceiling of the soft green leaves** literally "The man glanced up at the green gracious leaves."

454] **That wafted softly in the balm-borne breeze** literally "which wafted continuously such a light cool wind."

456] **Not a glimmer of glint, glances that man** literally "The size of a little mote shine upon the man."

461] **stopped** in the dialect sense of "stayed/resided." Literally "all around the lodge."

462] **And hankers for the same, when he's safe back home** literally "And wished it were in his country where he lived."

463] **Ephraim** a region in the middle of Israel. **Hermon Hills** a high mountain range in the north of Israel that borders on Lebanon and Syria. See maps in Appendix E.

470] **Zephyrus** the name in classical mythology for the west wind. Its most famous usage in Middle English is in line 3 of Chaucer's *The General Prologue to the Canterbury Tales*. **with blistering force** literally "that he breathes with warmth."

471] **scarf the sun's glare** literally "in front of the clear sun."

472] **Bare faced, she'll rise, and blaze like a torch** literally "Rise up broadly and burn like a candle."

476] **The sun had fried them before the prophet knew** literally "The bright sun had destroyed them before the man was aware."

477] **Then turned up the heat to burn even brighter** literally "And then heaved up the heat and burned fiercely."

479] **With his cover blown, he curls up and blubs** literally "The man grieved on the ground who had nowhere to hide."

481] **Sizzling with spleen, he shouts out irascibly** literally "He cries out heatedly with hot, violent anger."

485] **I'd just got settled, now all of that's scotched** literally "I'd found myself comfort which is now taken from me."

486] **My impressive canopy that kept me alive** literally "My majestic woodbine that covered my head."

488] **too jiggered to live** literally "I endure too long."

490] **to rant with such ignorance** literally "all your haughty noise."

494] **I want the earth to yawn open and swallow me up** literally "I wish I were wrapped in the earth of this world."

497] **precious** added in translation to reinforce the sense of Jonah's possessiveness and his neglect.

498] **at any point** literally "for the time of an hour."

499] **Here one minute and away the next** literally "It grew here in one moment and was away at another."

510–12] In the MS these lines follow 513–15. I have followed recent editorial practice, first suggested by Gollancz, in reversing the line ordering to retain a coherent ordering of the innocents.

510] **They can't fathom the difference of down and across** literally "Cannot discern between the upright of a ladder and the rung."

511] **Or reason how you reckon** literally "what rule operates mysteriously." I have transposed "left" here from line 513.

512] **Even if the consequences cost them their lives** literally "though his life should be lost on account of that."

514] **too overwrought** literally "that cannot distinguish."

515] **whatever the cost** literally "for all this high world."

516] **dozens** literally "many."

518] Why should I try those who return to Me literally "That may not sin in any situation to harm themselves."

519] Acknowledge Me literally "And come and know Me."

524] Quit grizzling and growling literally "Don't be so fierce, good man."

525–31] Opinions have differed as to where God's voice ends in the poem—and if it does. I have adopted the practice of recent critical editions in assigning lines 525–27 to God and lines 528–31 to the narrator.

528] So, if I'm skint, or in a scrape, or I've hit the skids literally "Therefore, when poverty oppresses me and many pains."

529] I must weather the storm—and with serenity literally "I must reconcile myself to it gently with sufferance."

530] The stiff upper lip is the ultimate proof literally "Therefore penance and pain prove clearly."

531] pip see note to line 1. **properly** literally "noble." Editors disagree whether "noble" is scribal or authorial. Its presence destroys the symmetry between the opening and closing lines of the poem. I have retained it as authorial, as the poet's capacity to wreck perfect symmetry is seen also in *Pearl*, where the concatenation breaks down between lines 720 and 721. Also, "noble" specifies that patience is aristocratic (see discussion in the Introduction, pp. 30–32). "properly" has the senses of "correctly," "elegantly, or in a fine manner," and, more colloquially, "very, or completely" (*OED* **properly** (adv)., 1, 5 and 6.

Appendix A: Scriptural Sources

[The first three extracts here are taken from the Douay-Rheims version of the Christian Bible. The English text is a close translation of the Latin Vulgate biblical text and is therefore the closest available version of the Bible that would have been known to the poet. The first extract is a complete text of the Old Testament story of Jonah. The second extract contains the eight Beatitudes delivered in Christ's Sermon on the Mount, recorded in the New Testament Gospel of Matthew. This corresponds to lines 13–28 of *Patience*. The third extract is taken from the Old Testament Book of Psalms, while the final selection is from the prophecy of Iunus (Jonah) in *The Qur'an*, Chapter 10. See discussion of the relevance of this in the Introduction, p. 36.]

1. The Old Testament Book of Jonah

Chapter 1

Now the word of the Lord came to Jonas the son of Amathi, saying: [2] Arise, and go to Ninive the great city, and preach in it: for the wickedness thereof is come up before me. [3] And Jonas rose up to flee into Tharsis from the face of the Lord, and he went down to Joppe, and found a ship going to Tharsis: and he paid the fare thereof, and went down into it, to go with them to Tharsis from the face of the Lord. [4] But the Lord sent a great wind into the sea: and a great tempest was raised in the sea, and the ship was in danger to be broken. [5] And the mariners were afraid, and the men cried to their god: and they cast forth the wares that were in the ship, into the sea, to lighten it of them: and Jonas went down into the inner part of the ship and fell into a deep sleep. [6] And the shipmaster came to him and said to him: Why art thou fast asleep? rise up, call upon thy God, if so be that God will think of us, that we may not perish. [7] And they said every-one to his fellow: Come, and let us cast lots, that we may know why this evil is upon us. And they cast lots, and the lot fell upon Jonas. [8] And they said to him: Tell us for what cause this evil is upon us, what is thy business? of what country art thou? and whither goest thou? or of what people art thou? [9] And he said to them: I am a Hebrew, and I fear the Lord the God of heaven, who made both the sea and the dry land. [10] And the men were greatly afraid, and they said to him: Why hast thou done this? (for the men knew that he fled from the face of the Lord: because he had told them.)

[11] And they said to him: What shall we do to thee, that the sea may be calm to us? for the sea flowed and swelled. [12] And he said to them: Take me up, and cast me into the sea, and the sea shall be calm to you: for I know that for my sake this great tempest is upon you. [13] And the men rowed hard to return to land, but they were not able: because the sea tossed and swelled upon them. [14] And they cried to the Lord, and said: We beseech thee, O Lord, let us not perish for this man's life, and lay not upon us innocent blood: for thou, O Lord, hast done as it pleased thee. [15] And they took Jonas, and cast him into the sea, and the sea ceased from raging.

[16] And the men feared the Lord exceedingly, and sacrificed victims to the Lord, and made vows.

Chapter 2

Now the Lord prepared a great fish to swallow up Jonas: and Jonas was in the belly of the fish three days and three nights. [2] And Jonas prayed to the Lord his God out of the belly of the fish. [3] And he said: I cried out of my affliction to the Lord, and he heard me: I cried out of the belly of hell, and thou hast heard my voice. [4] And thou hast cast me forth into the deep in the heart of the sea, and a flood hath compassed me: all thy billows, and thy waves have passed over me. [5] And I said: I am cast away out of the sight of thy eyes: but yet I shall see thy holy temple again.

[6] The waters compassed me about even to the soul: the deep hath closed me round about, the sea hath covered my head. [7] I went down to the lowest parts of the mountains: the bars of the earth have shut me up for ever: and thou wilt bring up my life from corruption, O Lord my God. [8] When my soul was in distress within me, I remembered the Lord: that my prayer may come to thee, unto thy holy temple. [9] They that are vain observe vanities, forsake their own mercy. [10] But I with the voice of praise will sacrifice to thee: I will pay whatsoever I have vowed for my salvation to the Lord.

[11] And the Lord spoke to the fish: and it vomited out Jonas upon the dry land.

Chapter 3

And the word of the Lord came to Jonas the second time, saying: [2] Arise, and go to Ninive the great city: and preach in it the preaching that I bid thee. [3] And Jonas arose, and went to Ninive, according to the word of the Lord: now Ninive was a great city of three days' journey. [4] And Jonas began to enter into the city one day's journey: and he cried, and said: Yet forty days, and Ninive shall be destroyed. [5] And the men of Ninive believed in God: and they proclaimed a fast and put on sackcloth from the greatest to the least. [6] And the word came to the king of Ninive; and he rose up out of his throne, and cast away his robe from him, and was clothed with sackcloth, and sat in ashes. [7] And he caused it to be proclaimed and published in Ninive from the mouth of the king and of his princes, saying: Let neither men nor beasts, oxen nor sheep, taste any thing: let them not feed, nor drink water. [8] And let men and beasts be covered with sackcloth, and cry to the Lord with all their strength, and let them turn everyone from his evil way, and from the iniquity that is in their hands. [9] Who can tell if God will turn, and forgive: and will turn away from his fierce anger, and we shall not perish? [10] And God saw their works, that they were turned from their evil way: and God had mercy with regard to the evil which he had said that he would do to them, and he did it not.

Chapter 4

And Jonas was exceedingly troubled, and was angry: [2] And he prayed to the Lord, and said: I beseech thee, O Lord, is not this what I said, when I was yet in my own country? therefore I went before to flee into Tharsis: for I know that thou art a gracious and merciful God, patient, and of much compassion, and easy to forgive evil. [3] And now, O Lord, I beseech thee take my life from me: for it is better for me to die than to live. [4] And the Lord said: Dost thou think thou hast reason to be angry? [5] Then Jonas went out of the city and sat toward the east side of the city: and he made himself a booth there, and he sat under it in the shadow, till he might see what would befall the city. [6] And the Lord God prepared an ivy, and it came up over the head of Jonas, to be a shadow over his head, and to cover him (for he was fatigued), and Jonas was exceeding glad of the ivy. [7] But God prepared a worm when the morning arose on the following day: and it struck the ivy and it withered. [8] And when the sun was risen, the Lord commanded a hot and burning wind: and the sun beat upon the head of Jonas, and he broiled with the heat: and he desired for his soul that he might die and said: It is better for me to die than to live. [9] And the Lord said to Jonas: Dost thou think thou hast reason to be angry, for the ivy? And he said: I am angry with reason even unto death. [10] And the Lord said: Thou art grieved for the ivy, for which thou hast not laboured, nor made it to grow, which in one night came up, and in one night perished. [11] And shall not I spare Ninive, that great city, in which there are more than a hundred and twenty thousand persons that know not how to distinguish between their right hand and their left, and many beasts?

2. Christ's Sermon on the Mount: The Beatitudes (Matthew 5:1–12)

And seeing the multitudes, he went up into a mountain, and when he was set down, his disciples came unto him. [2] And opening his mouth, he taught them, saying: [3] Blessed are the poor in spirit: for theirs is the kingdom of heaven. [4] Blessed are the meek: for they shall possess the land. [5] Blessed are they that mourn: for they shall be comforted. [6] Blessed are they that hunger and thirst after justice: for they shall have their fill. [7] Blessed are the merciful: for they shall obtain mercy. [8] Blessed are the clean of heart: for they shall see God. [9] Blessed are the peacemakers: for they shall be called children of God. [10] Blessed are they that suffer persecution for justice's sake: for theirs is the kingdom of heaven.

[11] Blessed are ye when they shall revile you, and persecute you, and speak all that is evil against you, untruly, for my sake: [12] Be glad and rejoice, for your reward is very great in heaven. For so they persecuted the prophets that were before you.

3. Psalm 68:2–10; 16–20

SAVE me, O God: for the waters are come in even unto my soul. [3] I stick fast in the mire of the deep: and there is no sure standing. I am come into the depth of the sea: and a tempest hath overwhelmed me. [4] I have laboured with crying; my jaws are become hoarse: my eyes have failed, whilst I hope in my God. [5] They are multiplied above the hairs of my head, who hate me without cause. My enemies are grown strong who have wrongfully persecuted me: then did I pay that which I took not away.

[6] O God, thou knowest my foolishness; and my offences are not hidden from thee: [7] Let not them be ashamed for me, who look for thee, O Lord, the Lord of hosts. Let them not be confounded on my account, who seek thee, O God of Israel. [8] Because for thy sake I have borne reproach; shame hath covered my face. [9] I am become a stranger to my brethren, and an alien to the sons of my mother. [10]

[...]

[16] Let not the tempest of water drown me, nor the deep swallow me up: and let not the pit shut her mouth upon me. [17] Hear me, O Lord, for thy mercy is kind; look upon me according to the

multitude of thy tender mercies. [18] And turn not away thy face from thy servant: for I am in trouble, hear me speedily. [19] Attend to my soul, and deliver it: save me because of my enemies. [20] Thou knowest my reproach, and my confusion, and my shame.

4. The Prophet Iunus, from the *Qur'an*, Chapter 10

Lo! those who believe and do good works, their Lord guideth them by their faith. Rivers will flow beneath them in the Gardens of Delight [9].

[…]

And when We cause mankind to taste of mercy after some adversity which had afflicted them, behold! they have some plot against Our revelations. Say: Allah is more swift in plotting. Lo! Our messengers write down that which ye plot. He it is Who maketh you to go on the land and the sea till, when ye are in the ships and they sail with them with a fair breeze and they are glad therein, a storm-wind reacheth them and the wave cometh unto them from every side and they deem that they are overwhelmed therein; (then) they cry unto Allah, making their faith pure for Him only: If Thou deliver us from this, we truly will be of the thankful. Yet when He hath delivered them, behold! they rebel in the earth wrongfully. O mankind! Your rebellion is only against yourselves. (Ye have) enjoyment of the life of the world; then unto Us is your return and We shall proclaim unto you what ye used to do [21–23].

[…]

Lo! Allah wrongeth not mankind in aught; but mankind wrong themselves [44].

[…]

If only there had been a community (of all those that were destroyed of old) that believed and profited by its belief as did the folk of Jonah! When they believed We drew off from them the torment of disgrace in the life of the world and gave them comfort for a while [99].

Appendix B: Analogues

[These three extracts are medieval versions of the Jonah story that use the Bible as a source. They enable us to compare the *Patience*-poet's treatment of the biblical story. The first extract is the Latin text of a poem written by Marbod of Rennes (c. 1035–1123), who was a teacher at the cathedral school of Angers in France and became its chancellor in 1069. He was appointed bishop of Rennes, Brittany, in 1096. Marbod composed numerous works in Latin, ranging from love poems, saints' lives, didactic verse, and hymns to a lapidary (an encyclopedia of the properties of stones and minerals). His poem about Jonah is edited by Alice Ahearne, who has emended the text where it is clearly in error. This is followed by Ahearne's translation of the Latin poem into modern English prose. This is the first time that the Latin text has been translated in full. The final selection is taken from a paraphrase of the Old Testament into Middle English metrical verse. The author of this huge enterprise is unknown, but it is thought that it was written in the last quarter of the fourteenth century and is, therefore, closely contemporary to the writing of *Patience*. We do not know with certainty that the *Patience*-poet knew either Marbod's work or the Middle English paraphrase, but there are some striking parallels and differences between the Latin poem and the metrical verse; these are discussed in the Introduction, pp. 16–17.]

1. *Naufragium Jonae Prophetae, Patrologia Latina* 171, cols. 1675–58. Edited by Alice Ahearne

Vos qui nescitis, nunc discite de Ninivitis;
Discite de Jona Dominum, fugiente propheta,
Qualiter est mersus, vel qualiter inde reversus.
Qui Dominum fugitis, pelagi discrimen aditis,
Quo sorbet vivos ballena Dei fugitivos.   5
Qui culpas fletis, magnum solamen habetis;
Non desperetis, quia cedent tristia laetis.
Tu qui delinquis, tu qui delicta relinquis,
Ex libro Jonae documenta tibi duo pone.
Lectio gestorum tibi sit delectio [directio] morum.   10

---

10. delectio] MS directio

Urbs ingens Ninive, multo celeberrima cive,
Divitiis opulens, regni diademate pollens,
Per turpem vitam Dominum commovit in iram.
Sed Deus iratus differt punire reatus;
15 Vult veniam quaeri, vult offensus misereri,
Ergo vocat Jonam, docet impendere ruinam
Urbi, sic meritae per turpia crimina vitae.
Surge meus vates, propriosque relinque penates;
Ad Niniven propera, refer illis propria verba.
20 Clama per vicos, terrendo meos inimicos:
Urbs evertetur citius quam quisque veretur,
Cives impuri sunt post modicum perituri.
Jonas surrexit; sed iter per devia flexit,
Ad mare descendit, dum Tharsum pergere tendit.
25 Non erat hoc jussum, tamen optat pergere Tharsum;
Sed profugum Domini fluctus tenuere marini.
O animum vatis mirandae simplicitatis!
Si procul esse putat Dominum sibi, dum loca mutat.
Qui complet totum nihil huic valet esse remotum.
30 Si petat infernum fugiens, regnumve supernum,
Stat Deus in tergo, fugiensque desinat ergo.
Sed juvat attendi quae causa fuit fugiendi.
Forte timens fatum, non ivit vaticinatum.
Nam quia portaret quod plebis corda gravaret,
35 Nuntius interitus, satis foret undique tritus,
Vel gladio stratus, vel forsitan igne crematus.
At non est fortis, qui sic timet ultima mortis,
Ut bene posse mori vitae postponat amori:
Nec Dominum credit, qui non sibi tutus obedit.
40 Ergo causa fugae non convenit ista prophetae.
Sed Dominum norat, quia nos revocare laborat,
Et cito condonat, si quis mala pristina ponat.
Nam cur praemunit, cur non cito crimina punit,
Cur jacet ante minas, nisi quod dare vult medicinas?
45 Territat aegrotum medicus, petat ut sibi potum.
Hoc timuit missus, quem conservavit abyssus,
Ne mentiretur, nisi dictum res sequeretur.
Diceret everti, quos sciret posse reverti,
Qui si rescirent, nulla ratione perirent.
50 Conscius ergo Dei fugit ora piae faciei,
Descendit Joppem, festinat scandere puppem.
Dimittit littus, quasi plus sic in aequore tutus.
Sed mare non nescit, quod fluctibus undique crescit

Cum rabie venti turbare viam fugienti.
Turbo rapit velum, tangit ratis ardua coelum,   55
Rursus ima cadit, metuendaque sub vada vadit.
Aer luce caret, neque sol, neque Cynthia paret,
Nec radiant stellae, sed nox fuit illa procellae;
Non paret ulla [sulus], fractus jacet in rate malus.
Dissiliunt remi, casus venit hora supremi,   60
Nautae suspirant, quos tanta pericula gyrant.
Praepositus navi liquit moderamina clavi.
Undique triste tonat, coelum fragor omne coronat.
Fulgura crebra micant, tanquam simul omnia dicant:
O fugitive redi, jussoque Tonantis obedi!   65
Haec Jonas nescit, pressusque sopore quiescit.
Interiora ratis sunt facta cubilia vatis.
Nauta sed accessit, pulsum pede voce lacessit.
Surge, quid est quod agis? multis dignissime plagis
Dormis securus, cum postmodo sis periturus: 70
Forsitan hac hora fluctu perit obruta prora.
Cum prece da fletum, fuget intercessio lethum,
Si poterit fieri, si non decet ultima fleri.
Interea ventis pelagique furore tumentis,
Exarmata ratis permiserat omnia fatis.   75
In mare jactatur quodcunque gravare putatur,
Nec tamen inde minus mergi timet anxia pinus:
Crimine namque gravis manet, et non pondere, navis;
Nec, quia culpa premit, levat hanc qui pondera demit.
Jam satis apparet, quamvis mala tanta pararet,   80
Iram divinam patet exagitare carinam.
Ergo reum mortis vestigat missio sortis,
Et trahit ad poenam captum sententia Jonam.
Mittitur in fluctus, cadit unda, caditque tumultus.
Iram Neptuni placat datus exitus uni.   85
Erigit absque mora sese gravis antea prora,
Causaque fit pacis submersio justa fugacis.
O recolenda satis, Deus, acta tuae pietatis!
Qui parcendo feris, et percutiens misereris,
Nosque fovere soles, quasi sit homo tua proles,   90
In regione maris, virtus bona, tu dominaris,
Et, sicut claret, mors ipsa tremens tibi paret
Mersum namque mari quis posse putet revocari?
Pisce quis absorptum remeare putabit ad ortum?

---

59. sulus] MS salus

95   Ecce venit cetus, maris alta secare suetus,
     Piscis par monti, saevissima bellua ponti,
     Et veluti praedam rapit absorbetque prophetam.
     Sed quasi commissum, nolit, velit, hunc dabit ipsum,
     Et feret invitus quem cepit ad utile littus.
100 Noctibus ergo tribus, totidemque propheta diebus,
     Ventre feri clausus, culpae gravis expiat ausus.
     Post haec, ad portum vomit insons bellua sortum,
     Qui simul evomitus, tetigit palpabile littus,
     Atque refulsit ei lux desperata diei.
105 Littora tam sivit, cupida quam mente petivit,
     Utque suam poenam damnat mare, damnat arenam,
     Tunc monitus rursum non audet flectere cursum;
     Sed tendit recta citus ad Ninivitica tecta:
     Utque moras nandi reparet mensura viandi,
110 Una luce tribus via curritur apta diebus.
     Moenibus intratis, ait ista viris sceleratis:
     Excidium Ninives vobis denuntio, cives,
     Clamor vestrorum petit aethera flagitiorum,
     Nec Deus haec ultra longum patietur inulta;
115 Post sex hebdomades urbem manet impia clades.
     Verba Dei coeli vobis loquor ore fideli.
     Territa gens istis, compuncta fit, anxia, tristis,
     Et mala quisque gemit quae per bona nulla redemit
     Saccis induti majores atque minuti,
120 Jejunaverunt, lacrymasque precesque dederunt
     Rex quoque quod fecit, fastus insignia jecit;
     Magnis quippe malis cessit decor imperialis,
     Et conturbatus pro cognitione reatus,
     Exemplo raro solio descendere claro
125 Non dedignatus, se planxit, et est lacrymatus.
     Tunc coram Jona deponitur alta corona,
     Imprimiturque [Imponiturque] cinis capiti, memoratio finis,
     Purpura projicitur, cilicinis rex operitur.
     Delicias coenae removet meditatio poenae,
130 Et vis moeroris fugat oblectamen odoris.
     Pluma fuit lecti tellus, sibi nescia flecti.
     Pro sonitu citharae suspiria moesta fuere,
     Et pro pigmentis miserae contritio mentis.
     Curia Magnatum fert consimilem cruciatum.
135 Aulicus et miles luctus imitantur heriles.

---

127. Imprimiturque] MS Imponiturque

Multus ubique cinis, nullusque caret cilicinis.
In moerore jacent, si forte [domnium] sibi placent.
Hinc vox praeconis loca pervolitans regionis,
Jussu regali cunctos monet ordine tali:
Omnis homo plangat, dolor anxius omne cor angat,   140
Et cibus et potus sit ab omni carne remotus.
Dum genitrix luget, nullus puer ubera suget.
Vox a jejunis resonabit stridula [curis].
Pabula jumentis nova cura negabit alentis.
Grex baculo flentis arcebitur ipse fluentis,   145
Clamet ut omne pecus, labor omnibus incubet aequus.
Quis scit an attritis parcat sententia mitis,
Ne quatiat quassos, ne figat vulnera passos?
Insuper occidat quos propria cura trucidat.
Non gaudet lenis miseros affligere poenis.   150
Non fit mansuetus miserorum sanguine laetus.
Tantis lamentis cessit furor Omnipotentis,
Suppliciis parcens, mortisque nefas procul arcens,
Et de Scripturis pia dans exempla futuris.

2. *The Prophet Jonah Lost at Sea.* Translated by Alice Ahearne

All you who do not know, learn now of the people of Nineveh; learn of Jonah, the prophet who fled from the Lord: how he was sunk in the sea, and how he came back again. All you who flee from the Lord, you are approaching the trial of the sea, where a whale swallows alive fugitives from God. All you who lament your sins, you have a great consolation; you should not despair, because sorrow will depart from you, and you will be joyful. You who do wrong, and you who abandon wrongdoing, consider for yourself the two examples from the Book of Jonah. [10] Let the teaching of what was done be the choice [lit. guidance] of your conduct.

 The huge city of Nineveh, enormously populated with countless citizens, glittering with wealth, mighty in its rule of the kingdom, has aroused the Lord to anger by its wicked way of life. But God, though angry, defers punishing the wrongdoers; He wishes for mercy to be sought, He wishes to pardon their transgressions. So He calls to Jonah and informs him that destruction is hanging over the city, deserving of this as it is for the wicked sins of its way of life. "Arise, my prophet, leave behind your own household [gods]; make haste to Nineveh, convey a special message to them. [20] Shout throughout the streets,

---

137. domnium] MS Dominum
143. curis] MS cunis

to terrify those hostile to me: the city will be overthrown faster than anyone fears; the citizens, impure beyond measure, will die."

Jonah has arisen; but he has changed his course through detours, and comes down to the sea, aiming to press on to Tarshish. This is not what was ordered, yet he chooses to make for Tarshish. But the waves of the sea hold back the fugitive of the Lord.

Oh, of what astonishing simplicity is the mind of the prophet, if he thinks the Lord is far from him, just because he changes his location! Even if he travels the whole world, he has no power to be apart from Him. [30] If in his flight he seeks Hell, or the kingdom of Heaven, still God stands on his back, and so he should desist from flight.

But it is helpful to consider what the reason was for his fleeing. Perhaps he did not go because he feared his death was foretold. For because he would be bringing what would burden the hearts of the people, a messenger of destruction, he would be utterly beaten from all sides, either laid low by the sword, or perhaps burnt at the stake. But anyone who so fears the final end of death that they esteem the chance to die well less than love of life is not strong; nor does anyone who does not obey the Lord to stay safe believe in Him.

[40] So this reason for flight is not right for a prophet. But he knew the Lord, knew that He strives to redeem us, and He swiftly grants forgiveness, if anyone should abandon their former wickedness. For why does He protect us, why does He not swiftly punish our sins, why does He stop at threats, unless He wishes to give the remedy? The doctor terrifies the sick patient, so that they beg for the healing draught. It was this that the emissary feared that once the sea delivered him safely, he might be lying, if things did not turn out as he said. He might say that they would be destroyed, those whom he knew could be redeemed, and then if they were to come to their senses, they would not perish for any reason.

[50] And so, knowing God, he flees His face of holy aspect; he goes down to Jaffa and hastens to board a ship. He bids farewell to the land, as if he will be any safer thus at sea.

But the sea is not unaware, and swells with waves on all sides in a fury of wind to churn up the route for the fugitive. The storm tears away the sail, the ship rises up high and touches the sky, then falls back down deep, and strays into the dreaded shallows. The sky has lost its light, neither sun nor moon are there, no stars shine; there is only the darkness of the storm. There is no [safety] in sight, and the mast lies splintered on the deck. [60] The oarsmen are deserting; the final hour of death has come. The sailors are whimpering, whirled around by such great dangers. The helmsman has abandoned control of the tiller. On all sides it thunders fearfully; the crashing echoes around the whole sky. Lightning-bolts flash one after another, and it is just as if everything is saying, "Go back, fugitive, obey the command of the Thunderer!"

Of all this Jonah is unaware—he is resting, weighed down by sleep. The prophet's bed has been made up below decks. But a sailor comes up, kicks him, lashes him with his voice: "Get up, what are you doing? You deserve a good beating! [70] You sleep easy, when very soon you might perish! Perhaps at this very moment the ship is lost, scuppered by the waves. Make lamentations and prayers, let your intercession put death to flight, if it can be so, if it is not the right time to bewail our end!"

Meanwhile the ship, stripped bare by the winds and the fury of the swelling sea, has committed everything to fate. Whatever is thought to weigh it down is scattered into the sea, but even then its timber is no less fearful of being sunk: for the ship remains heavy with a sin, and not with freight; nor, because wrongdoing presses it down, can anyone lighten it by jettisoning cargo.

[80] Now it is clear enough, although He is bringing about such great evils, that it is divine anger that assails the ship. So the casting of a lot marks out the wrongdoer for death, and the judgement hauls up the captured Jonah for punishment. He is cast into the sea. At once the waves cease, and the pandemonium subsides. The ruin inflicted on one man appeases the wrath of Neptune. The ship, heavy before, raises itself up away from its hindrance, and the just submersion of the fugitive becomes the cause of peace.

O God, how much Your acts of mercy should be remembered! You who smite by being merciful, and are merciful as You smite, [90] You are accustomed also to cherish us, as if humankind were Your offspring. In the region of the sea, You, benign power, have dominion, and, clear as day, death itself can be seen trembling before You. For who would think someone plunged into the sea could be summoned back? Who will think someone swallowed by a fish will come back to the daylight?

Behold, here comes the whale—accustomed to reaping the depths of the sea, a fish as big as a mountain, the most savage monster of the sea—and he snaps up the prophet like prey and swallows him. But whether he wants to or not, he will yield him up, as if entrusted to him, and though unwilling, will bear the man he caught to the right shore.

[100] So for three nights and as many days, the prophet, imprisoned in the belly of the beast, atones for the grave sin he attempted. After this, without harming him, the monster brings him back up and spits him out towards the harbour. The moment he is spat out, he has touched solid land, and the despaired-of light of day shines

for him again. He leaves the shore as eagerly as he sought it, and condemns both sea and sand as his punishment.

He has learned his lesson. He dares not change his course again, but at once makes straight for the homes of Nineveh; and so that the duration of his travelling should make up for the delays of his swim, [110] a journey that should take three days is run in one. Once within the walls, he says this to the wicked people: "I announce to you your ruin, citizens of Nineveh! The clamour of your outrages is reaching the heavens, and God will not suffer these to go unavenged much longer; after six weeks, ungodly destruction falls on the city. With faithful lips I speak to you the word of God in Heaven."

Terrified by this, the people become remorseful, uneasy, aggrieved, and each bewails the sins which they can redeem by no good acts. Greater and lesser citizens alike are clad in sackcloth, [120] they have begun to fast, and to give tears and prayers.

The king too has done this, has discarded his marks of pride; indeed, his royal finery has desisted from its great evils, and, greatly perturbed by the recognition of his guilt, in a rare demonstration, he has not disdained to come down from his distinguished throne, and he has beaten his breast and wept. Then, in the presence of Jonah, the lofty crown is laid down and ash is pressed (f. placed) onto his head, a reminder of the final end. His purple robes are thrown out, and the king is swathed in goatskin. Reflection on the punishment takes away the pleasures of sin, [130] and the strength of grief puts to flight the delight of luxury. His feather bed is now the ground, which knows nothing of softness. In place of the music of the lyre there are sad sighs, and instead of bright colours there is the gloomy regret of the wretched mind.

The council of great men bears a similar torture. The courtier and the soldier emulate their ruler's grieving attire. Copious ash is everywhere, no one is without their goatskin. They languish in misery, in case by any chance they might reconcile the Lord to them. After this, the voice of a herald, winging through all the districts of the city, instructs them all by royal decree with this commandment:

[140] "Let everyone beat their breast, let uneasy anguish grip every heart, and let food and drink be distant from every living thing. While the mother is grieving, no child shall suckle her breasts. A wailing voice will resound from starving [cradles]. The farmer's new care will deny fodder to the beasts of burden. The very flock shall be kept back from the streams by the grieving shepherd's staff, so that the whole herd bellows, so that the same hardship lies on all.

"Who knows whether a lenient judgement may spare us when we are ground down, or may strike us when we have been struck, or transfix us when we have already suffered wounds? Or if it may kill too those whose own worries torment them?"

[150] He is mild and does not rejoice in striking the wretched with punishments. He is gentle and does not become joyful at the blood of the wretched. At such great lamentations, the wrath of the Almighty has subsided, sparing His suppliants, keeping far off the abomination of death, and setting examples of godliness from the Scriptures yet to be.

3. From the Middle English Metrical Paraphrase of the Book of Jonah, translated from *A Middle English Metrical Paraphrase of the Old Testament*, edited by Urban Ohlander (Almqvist and Wiksell, 1960), vol. 3, pp. 124–28, lines 13836–4004

Now is it time to tell of God's powerful actions toward men, and of the great wonders that happened to his prophet called Jonah; and how God told him that day and night the people of Nineveh rebelled against his teaching. In order to correct them he commanded Jonah to go and preach to those people morning and evening, so they were not lost. (13836–48)

Jonah had heard about Nineveh and how its people were so wicked; sinners in every kind, and he was afraid to go there. He found sailors who were travelling overseas and made arrangements as quickly as he could to go to some far country so that he and God would never meet again. When he behaved so stupidly, it was from wicked foolishness. God is omnipotent and from him may nothing be hidden. (13849–60)

He met right away with mariners who said they were sailing to Sicily. He promised them good wages to take them to that foreign island. But when they were set sail on the sea, many miles from land, such storms blew up and battered them they thought they would be lost in no time. The merchants amongst them threw many rich items overboard, but the storm was so strong they had no hope they would survive. (13861–72)

So when they found themselves in such dire circumstances, fearing that they would never escape the danger, they took counsel and cast lots, and straightaway the lot fell to Jonah. They accosted him where he lay on a bed and asked him what he had done. He said, "I fled from God and all this torment is because of me. I acknowledge my guilt to God, and all my wicked thoughts. It is better that I die, rather than those who have committed no sin." (13873–84)

When they heard this, they were sorry that his life would last no longer, but because there was no other remedy, they threw him into the sea and then sailed fast to their own country. And Jonah was immediately swallowed by a whale, but without any damage to bones or flesh. He spent three days and three nights inside the whale. In such a way God shows his power over his friends. (13885-96)

When three days and three nights were past, the fish brought him to a bank and left him there alone in the land which God had told him to seek in the first place. Jonah wept and lamented and knew that he had behaved foolishly. And then God caught him and told him his message, "Go into Nineveh and announce to everyone that both they and their city will be sunk on account of their sin (13897-908)

Within forty days unless they pray and perform penance to my satisfaction." Then Jonah went quickly on his way; he dared make no further delay. It is said that that city was so vast and broad in its paths that a man could scarcely traverse it within three days. Jonah entered in as God had instructed him and began to preach to them. He said to them: (13909-20)

"Your Saviour has sent me to warn you of his intentions. Unless you will amend your wicked ways and pledge to grieve God no further, before 40 days have passed, you shall be beset with terrible misery and agony. Your city will sink to Hell like the five others before you. They practised abhorrent sins, just as you do now. Trust me, unless you change, your city sinks," he says. (13921-32)

Then he stalked away from that city and the people prayed diligently and did penance. He settled himself down under a hill to see what would happen next. And he gazed constantly on that city waiting for it to sink as God had said it would. And because it was still standing, he was furious with anger, but God was satisfied with their penance, and therefore they had their wish. Jonah was very displeased with the heat of the full sun. (13969-80)

And yet, in the summer season it happened that God (who can bring all blessings), made a green ivy to grow that sheltered Jonah completely. So he sat between two hills knowing full well that all would be destroyed. He said to himself in anger, "this business is dishonest, I am convinced of it." But in the morning at prime, his astonishment was even greater. The sun had no clouds before it and his ivy had vanished. (13969-92)

Then he was in anguish that his plant had disappeared overnight. God said to him "why do you grieve for something over which you have no power? It pleases me now to save the people of Nineveh because they are fully repentant." Then he said, "Lord, now think of me, that I might soon be dashed to death and depart this life." Thus we leave these matters and pick up from where we left off to end The Book of Kings. (13993-4004)

Appendix C: Other Contemporary Contexts

[All translations in this appendix are by Helen Barr.]

1. Wycliffite Sermon for All Saints' Day (Matthew 5.1:12), translated from *English Wycliffite Sermon 68*: "In Die Omnium Sanctorum" (On All Saints' Day), edited by Pamela Gradon (U of Oxford P, 1988), pp. 320–27

[This first extract is from a lengthy cycle of sermons composed in the late fourteenth century by followers of the teachings of the Oxford philosopher John Wyclif (c. 1320–84). At the most radical end of Wycliffite thought was the belief that the institutional Church on earth was corrupt and unnecessary. Only God could forgive sin, and the True Church was the congregation of those elected for salvation in heaven. This anonymous sermon was written to accompany the gospel reading from Matthew for All Saints' Day that is paraphrased in *Patience*, lines 13–28. In the poem, there is no mention of persecution in the rendering of the eighth Beatitude. The sermon glosses biblical persecution as the hounding of true Christian preachers by the contemporary institutional Church named here, and elsewhere in Lollard texts, as the Church of Antichrist.]

But poverty of spirit stands in meekness; when a man knows the Maker above, how He is rich without end, and we are poor beggars, and puts himself meekly under the ordinance of God. Whatever God ordains for his servant, in deed, or suffering, his servant considers himself well pleased since God is an ironsmith, and he is his instrument. He is ready, wherever God makes him a hammer, tongs, or an anvil, to suffer in any way that God wills. And certainly, none come to heaven unless he is pliable in this way, for an ironsmith forges his metal only if it will be tempered. And this virtue lasts both here and in heaven (lines 27–37).

[…]

Christ tells in the fourth saying, "*Blessed are they that hunger and thirst after righteousness, for they shall be baptised in the bliss of heaven.*" … For, if we think on God's law, and especially how priests defile God's ordinance, turning again to the sins of the flesh, the devil, and the world, a just man should hunger and thirst for the righteous punishment of such men. I cannot see any desire here on earth greater than the pursuit of this righteousness: to wish that Christ's ordinance were fulfilled in number, weight, and measure that Christ ordained for his church. And that his priests should always be poor in spirit.

For the estate of priests is more worldly than the estate of knight. We must dread that pride will follow, with avarice and lechery and abandonment of the duties that Christ commanded his priests to perform. And so, in the place of shepherds who should teach the way to heaven, the church is full of wolves that bring men down and lead them to hell. For Christ's ordinance was righteous, and particularly with regard to the poverty of priests, even if now the new sects say that Christ's ordinance was noxious poison. Lords should reflect on this, and labour to amend it. Otherwise they shall not be baptised in heaven through the bliss of the limbs of Christ (98–118).

[...]

The eighth, and last, saying that Christ said on this matter runs: they are blessed who suffer persecution, for theirs is the Kingdom of Heaven by right, as it is of those first men [those poor in spirit]. For the man that is persecuted to death for defending righteousness has some sight of bliss and some indication of security. And so he has here in shackles, bliss that is different from others, and as men commonly say, such men pass into heaven without suffering.

And because this [willingness to suffer persecution] is a necessary virtue, and harder than the others, so the reward is well matched to it. For sure, if men would stand resolute, and move with one accord for righteousness, the devil's party would be completely feeble, and men would have peace and live well. And so it is vital to encourage many to practise this virtue. For many are traitors to God and officers of the devil, in secret, or openly, and will not stand up for God's law.

That is why Christ applies these words especially to his apostles and teaches them that the persecution that men dread most here on earth should be comfortable for those who stand up for God's law. *Blessed shall ye be, says Christ, when men shall curse you, and when men shall persecute you, and shall speak all manner of evil against you on my account. Rejoice and be glad for the terms of hire are great in heaven.* And this saying encourages many men to stand against Antichrist, for he will curse men zealously and persecute them as heretics. However (truthfully), those who are cursed are those who fear persecution and abandon the preaching of God's law and his will (166–89).

2. From Dan Michel, *Ayenbite of Inwit or Remorse of Conscience*, edited by Richard Morris, EETS OS 23 (1866)

[The following three extracts are taken from a pastoral manual written by Dan Michel (fl. 1340s), a monk from Canterbury. In 1215, an international meeting of the Church known as the Lateran Council decreed that the clergy should undertake extensive pastoral instruction of lay people. From this point onwards there was steady growth in the production of works in English written to promote Christian doctrine, practices, and values. Dan Michel was a vibrant translator of a work written initially in French. Similar interpretations of the virtue of patience can be found in other pastoral manuals written in the later fourteenth/early fifteenth centuries such as *Handling Synne*, *Vices and Virtues*, *Jacob's Well*, and *The Pricke of Conscience*. The manuals were written primarily for the instruction of parish clergy, who in turn would educate their parishioners by using material from these manuals in sermons, catechisms, or hearing confessions.]

a. From the Virtue of Prowess: The Fourth Degree, Patience, p. 167

Just as the Holy Ghost strengthens his knight to endure the torments and the sorrows that are to yet come, so he makes him strong and resilient to suffer them when they arrive. And that is the fourth degree that is called patience, or endurance. Through this virtue a man or woman defeats their enemies: the world, the flesh and the devil and all that they may do or say. Patience is the shield of gold that for the love of God protects them on all sides, as the Psalter says, so that no blow may hurt their hearts. This virtue belongs only to those who have been tempted; for as Saint Paul says, "just as the fire makes the tile hard, without this virtue is no-one tested; no more than gold can be refined without fire. For without endurance no man or woman may come to perfection; without patience, no-one can be victorious, for whoever cannot endure is defeated."

We see examples of this in hand-crafted works. The gold or silver cup suffers frequent fire and many blows before it is set upon the king's table; likewise a chalice before it is worthy to be placed upon the altar. A barrel suffers a great many blows before it is filled with wine or ale, a scarlet cloth is foully besmirched by feet before the queen gets to wear it. You can find as many examples of such things as you can find crafts in Paris. For through this virtue a man or woman is as strong as the iron that tempers all other metals. It is as precious as gold, for the more fire it endures, the finer it becomes. It is brighter and softer than the cricket that lives in the fire, and it nourishes and bathes the fish that endure in mighty waters full of tempest and tribulations.

b. From the Sin of Sloth, pp. 33–34

There are six causes of sloth that are evil and lead to damnation. One is disobedience: when a man will not perform the penance he has been asked to do, or if he is charged with a duty, and it seems to him too difficult, he excuses himself, or if he does undertake it, he does very little of it, or even nothing at all.

The second cause of sloth is unwillingness to suffer. Just as he has no stamina as a result of disobedience, neither has he the resilience to suffer because of impatience. Impatience is unwillingness to suffer, and as a result no man dare speak to him to warn him of the dangers to his soul.

The third is grouching. When another person speaks of his well-being, he gets angry and grouches. It seems to him that the speaker despises him and he is consumed by wrath, which is the fourth vice. So furiously does his anger take hold of him, that whatever any good person says to him, does to him, and everything that he hears and sees vexes him. As a result he is overcome by sadness and self-hatred and wishes to die. And that is the fifth vice.

c. From the Sins of the Tongue, p. 68

Grouching against God has many more causes [than against fellow men]. For when a man loses the hope of grace and cannot endure, he thinks himself above God. Whatever God does in this world, if it is not to his liking, straightaway he complains against God and sings the Lord's Prayer. But it is not the Lord's prayer, but the devil's; for just as the Holy Ghost teaches his chosen ones to sing the holy song of heaven in their hearts, that is "Deo Gracias—may God be worthily thanked for all that he does for us, and sends us," so does the wicked fiend make his disciples sing the song of hell, composed of infernal grouching for eternity, unless God does everything that suits them.

Indeed, a man is a mighty fool, and mad, if he wants God to give account of everything He does. If He sends him anger and tribulation, poverty, sickness, bitter tears, rain, drought, or if he gives a lot to one person, and nothing to another, unless this is done according to his own choosing, then he turns on God, rails at him with bitter spite.

Is it any wonder, then, that God wreaks vengeance on such people who want to rob him of his sovereignty and of his patience?

3. The Storm Scene from *The Gest Hystoriale of the Destruction of Troy*, edited by G.A. Panton and D. Donaldson, EETS OS 39, 56 (1869, 1874), 2 vols.

[Late medieval English alliterative poetry was well suited to the composing of dramatic scenes. Using a poetic device known as "catalogue," poets could heap up detail after sensory detail to produce verse of great charge and animation. The catalogue could be put to various uses—descriptions of nature, clothing, buildings, and artefacts—and is used in several poems to describe storms. The extract below offers comparison with the storm scenes in *Patience*.

The Destruction of Troy is an English poetic translation by John Clerk of the Latin prose *Historia Destructionis Troiae* (History of the Destruction of Troy), written by Guido delle Colonne (c. 1215–c. 1290). The precise date of Clerk's English poem is unknown, but it is generally thought to have been written in the late fourteenth century. At sixteen thousand lines, it is the longest surviving Middle English alliterative poem.]

Book XXXI, lines 12463–518

By fortune it fell that the fairest of the year	
Had passed to the pitch of pale-faced winter.	
Harvest, with its heat, the sun high in the sky,	12465
Changed into chill, sun's chariot swung low.	
Tempests had torn the leaves from the trees.	
Birds abandoned their chirpy ballades.	
The wind from the west had awoken.	
It blew great blasts o'er the broad waves.	12470
Huge black clouds cloaked clear air	
With the murkiest of mists, mizzled with showers.	
Floods rose furiously as the rainfall persisted	
As winter woke up with his drench-wet air.	
The great navy of the Greeks and their gilded kings	12475
Put together a plan to depart from the town,	
The lords longed sorely to see their own lands,	
So deep was their desire, they didn't doubt the weather,	

	Careless for the season's inclement storms
12480	And the dangers destined from the dingy waves,
	They were blighted by bad luck in the blink of an eye,
	For many mighty lords their mission was shot.
	The pining princes pelted to the shore,
	Many shining knights rushed onto ships
12485	With the treasure of the Trojans they had taken before:
	Heaps of hoards of heirlooms and spoils.
	The course of the cold sea and the skies above
	Were as calm as could be considering the winter,
	They hauled out to sea and hoisted their sails,
12490	And left the bank with strong blasts at their back.
	For four days and four nights they fared without harm,
	Sailed in safety with seasonable winds.
	But the fifth day was fierce as is fitting for winter.
	Without warning the wind went from breeze to gale,
12495	Mist and murk milled with the wind
	Thunder and thick rain threw the skies awry,
	With blood-curdling cracklings, chaos unleashed,
	The firmament flashed in fire,
	No light but the lash of the lightning zags
12500	That skittered through the skies with screaming blaze
	Through clashes of clouds close to the heavens.
	The firmament seemed on fire the heat was so fierce.
	The ferocious force of the fearsome wind
	Whipped up the waves to the woebegone hills,
12505	The violent storm vied with the sail-vessels—
	They tottered at the top of the tallest waves,
	As the unleashed sea scattered the ships,
	Rode rough-shod, unruly, over the waves
	And dispersed the people—painful to see—
12510	Into countries uncouth. It cut down their sails,
	Ripped up their ropes, wrenched open their hatches,
	Collapsed the top-castles and unloosed their tackle.
	Nightfall brought more noxious news.
	The entire entourage of the eminent King Telamon,
12515	With their shining ships and their shimmering goods
	Were burnt in the sea by the blazing light,
	The dazzling dart that dived from the heavens
	Drowned indiscriminately the doughty and the weak.

4. The Whale from the Middle English *Physiologus*, translated from *The Middle English Physiologus*, edited by Hanneke Wirtjes, EETS, OS 299 (1991), lines 335–90

[The *Physiologus* was originally a Greek text written probably in the second century CE. It was translated into various languages in the Middle Ages, including Latin, Old English, and Middle English. The *Physiologus* catalogues the moral and symbolic qualities of animals, plants, minerals, and fantastical creatures.]

Its nature

The whale is a fish	335
In water, the biggest that exists,	
So massive you would boast	
If you saw it when it floats	
It was an island	
Resting on the sea ground.	340
This fish is a violent jotun [i.e., giant],	
When he's hungry, his mouth gapes open,	
And from his throat there speeds a breath	
More fragrant than any earthly scent	
Which makes the other fish swim to him	345
And sends them into delirium.	
They come and swirl in his mouth so sweet,	
Completely ignorant of his deceit.	
This whale then clamps fast his jaws	
And sucks the fishes into his maw,	350
Thus he cons the smaller fish,	
But the largest don't fall for this conjuring trick.	
This fish dwells at the bottom of the sea	
In rude health—contentedly—	
Until the time comes	355
When the sea is whipped by storms.	
When summer and winter collide	
No longer there may he reside.	
The abyss is so turbid,	
His haven's disturbed.	360
He rises up and floats immobile	
All the while the weather's hostile.	
Sailors battered by waves and sky	
Are dying to live; they don't want to die.	
They look around; the fish they spy and	365

Think the jotun is an island
Which warms their hearts with such delight
They row there fast with all their might.
The sailors moor
370 And step on shore.
With flint and stone they kindle tinder
To build a fire upon this wonder
To warm them through and eat and drink.
The fish feels the flames and makes them sink.
375 He dives at once to the murky depths
And without a mark on their flesh, settles their deaths.

Its meaning

The devil's so skilled at evil tricks
His crafts resemble those of witches.
He causes men to hunger and thirst
380 For every sin—especially the worst.
He draws men in with perfumed breath
And whoever gets drawn gets lasting death.
Those who are little, their faith is flighty,
But he has no mastery over the mighty.
385 By mighty I mean the steadfast shoal
Who truly believe in body and soul.
Anyone who listens to the devil's fables
Will find in the end he turns the tables.
Anyone who fastens hope on the whale
390 Will follow him down to the pit of hell.

Appendix D: Visual Materials

1. The illustrations to *Patience* in BL MS Cotton Nero A.x

[Written texts in the Middle Ages were nourished by a rich visual tradition of iconography and symbols. Illustration 1 shows the pictures in BL MS Cotton Nero A.x that accompany the text of *Patience*.]

Fol.86r   Fol.86v

PATIENCE   113

2. The whale as island from Gerald of Wales's *Topographia Hibernica* (Salisbury, late twelfth–early thirteenth century), Harley MS 4751, f. 69r

[Gerald of Wales (1146–1223) was an influential churchman during the reign of Henry II (r. 1154–89). His *Topographia Hibernica* (c. 1188) is an account of the landscape and people of Ireland. The first part of the work describes the landscape, flora, and fauna and is accompanied in the Harley manuscripts by illustrations.]

3. A whale opens its mouth and lets out a sweet scent to lure small fish, in a bestiary (England, second or third quarter of the thirteenth century), British Library Sloane MS 3544, f. 42v

[A bestiary was a catalogue of the properties of the natural world that derives in part from the *Physiologus* tradition. The moral and symbolic properties of animals, fish, and birds were often illustrated. This page from the British Library Sloan manuscripts illustrates the whale/devil's deceptive sweet breath recounted in the *Physiologus*.]

4. The Annunciation: The Holy Spirit as Dove Flies into Mary's Ear, Manuscript Illumination with the Annunciation in an Initial R, from a Gradual, Lake Constance, Switzerland (c. 1300), https://www.metmuseum.org/art/collection/search/466086

[Christian iconography was international. This illustration is from a gradual (a chant or hymn in the sung in the Mass). It is a particularly graphic iconographical representation of God's announcement to the Virgin Mary that she will conceive His Son. The dove represents God's Holy Spirit. It flies into Mary's ear to show that she is still a Virgin when she conceives Christ. Lines 63–64 of *Patience*, which describe God speaking brusquely and directly into Jonah's ear, are a cheeky tweak on this iconographical tradition.]

116 APPENDIX D: VISUAL MATERIALS

5. Doom Painting in the Church of Thomas à Becket, showing kings and a bishop and other sinners pulled into the mouth of hell by demons (Salisbury, fifteenth century), https://www.wiltshirehistoricchurchestrust.org.uk/church/trail-1-in-and-around-the-city-of-salisbury/st-thomas-becket-salisbury/

[Before the Reformation, medieval parish churches were often richly decorated with wall paintings. The chancel arch that separated the chancel (the place of the clergy) from the nave (the place of the laity) was painted with a representation of the Last Judgement. The laity would see before them a representation of their ultimate spiritual fate. God was depicted top centre. The saved souls were to his right, and those who were damned to his left. The sinners are gobbled into the mouth of hell, figured as the gaping jaws of a whale's mouth. This wall painting shows bishops and kings among the damned and resonates strongly with the description of the whale's stomach in *Patience*, with its implicit criticism of church and nobility (267–80). The damned are shown dragged into hell on a chain pulled by demons. This iconographical detail informs *Patience* line 270, where Jonah is described being reeled into the whale's stomach by a rope.]

Appendix E: Sketch Maps of the Topography of Patience

[As discussed in the Introduction, the poet creates a complex geography of the holy land from the places that he names in the poem—not all of them present in the biblical book of Jonah. The territorial geography of the Old Testament is conflated with that of the New Testament without specific location in time. I have drawn these sketch maps to illustrate the difficulties of plotting the geography of *Patience*. Territorial claims to possession, and the naming of the lands in this region, are ongoing. The third map shows Jonah's attempted route were he to have been successful in sailing to Tarshish, which is in the opposite direction from Nineveh.]

1. Old Testament

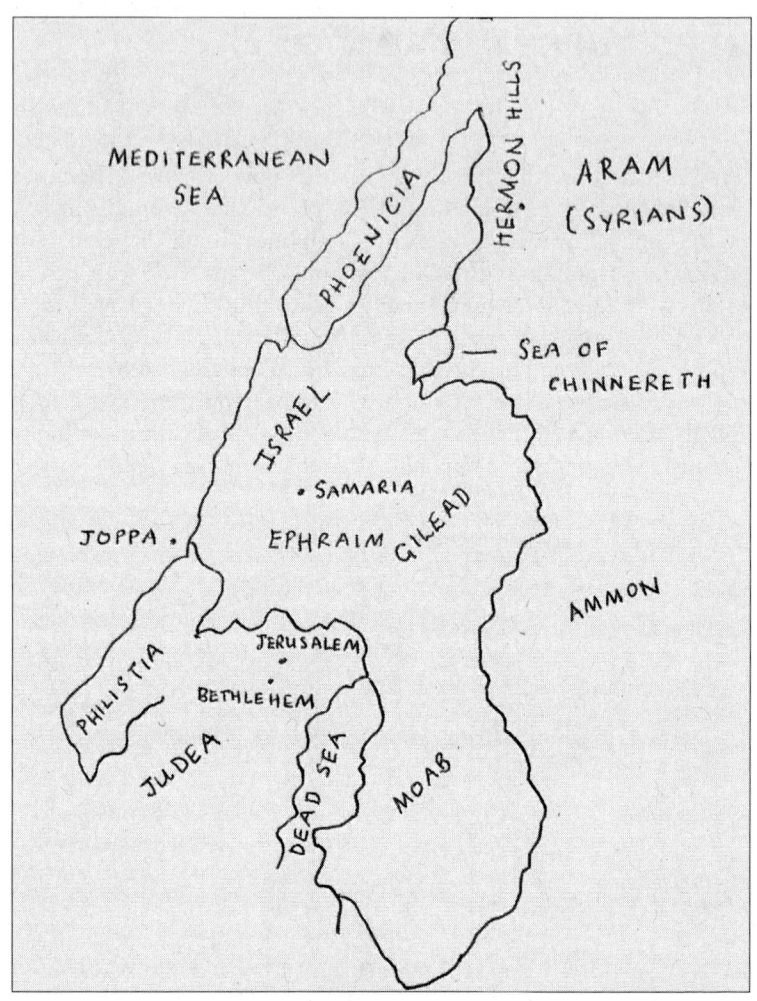

120 APPENDIX E: SKETCH MAPS OF THE TOPOGRAPHY OF *PATIENCE*

2. New Testament

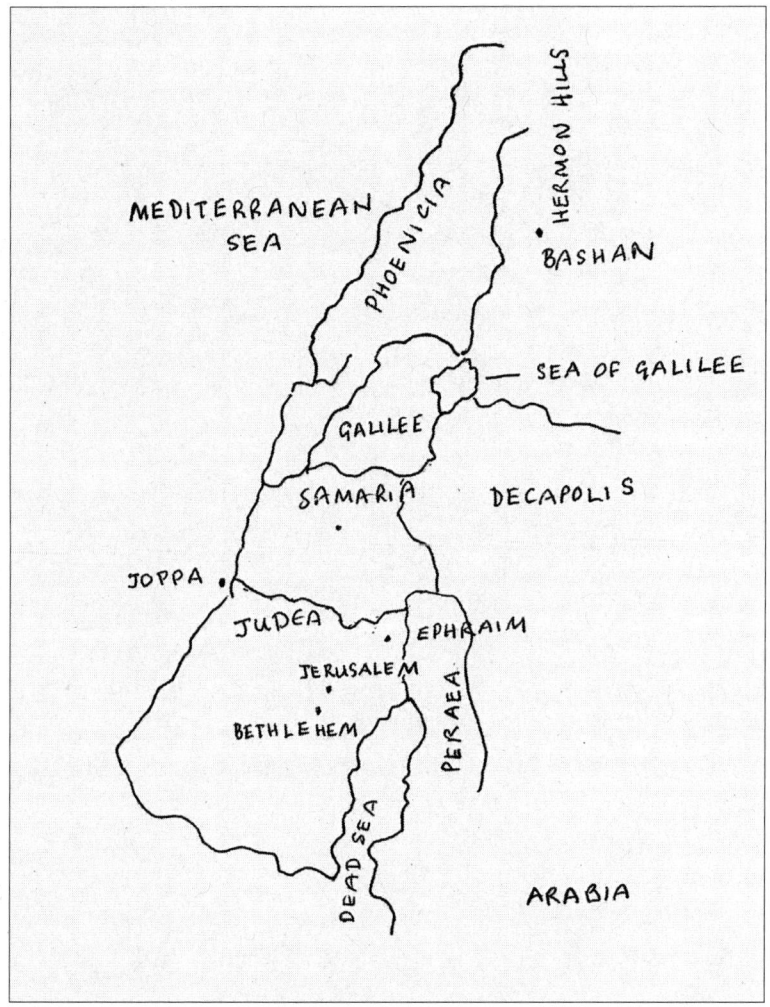

3. Jonah's Journey

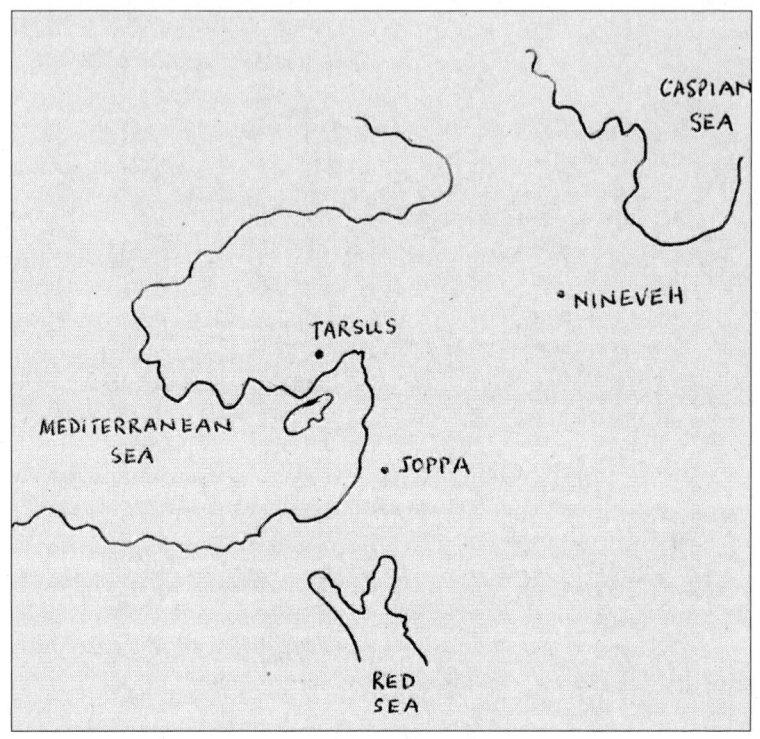

Works Cited and Recommended Reading

Editions of *Patience*

A Book of Middle English. Edited by J.A. Burrow and Thorlac Turville-Petre. 3rd ed., Blackwell, 2005.
The Complete Works of the Pearl *Poet*. Edited by Casey Finch et al. U of California P, 1993.
Early English Alliterative Poems. Edited by Richard Morris. EETS O.S. 1., 1869.
The Gawain Poet: Complete Works. Edited by Marie Borroff. W.W. Norton, 2011.
Patience. Edited by J.J. Anderson. U of Manchester P, 1977.
Patience, an Alliterative Version of Jonah by the Poet of Pearl. Edited by Israel Gollancz. Oxford UP, 1913.
Pearl, Cleanness, Patience, Sir Gawain and the Green Knight. Edited by A.C. Cawley and J.J. Anderson. Dent, 1976.
The Pearl Poems: An Omnibus Edition. Edited by William Vantuono. 2 vols., Garland, 1984.
The Poems of the Pearl Manuscript. Edited by Malcolm Andrew and Ronald Waldron. 5th ed., U of Exeter P, 2007.
The Poems of the Pearl Manuscript in Modern English Prose Translation. Translated by Malcolm Andrew and Ronald Waldron. U of Exeter P, 2008.
Sir Gawain and the Green Knight; Patience; and Pearl, Verse Translations. Translated by Marie Borroff. W.W. Norton, 2000.
The Works of the Gawain Poet: Pearl, Cleanness, Patience, Sir Gawain and the Green Knight. Edited by Ad Putter and Myra Stokes. Penguin, 2014.

Other Primary Texts

The Book of Vices and Virtues: A Fourteenth Century English Translation of the Somme Le Roi of Lorens D'Orléans. Edited by W. Nelson Francis. EETS OS 217, 1942.
Chaucer, Geoffrey. *The Riverside Chaucer*. Edited by L.D. Benson et al., 3rd ed., Oxford UP, 2008.
de Lorris, Guillaume, and Jean de Meun. *The Romance of the Rose*. Translated by Charles Dahlberg, 3rd ed., Princeton UP, 1995.

English Wycliffite Sermons. Edited by Pamela Gradon. Vol. 2, Oxford UP, 1988.
The Gest Hystoriale of the Destruction of Troy. Edited by G.A. Panton and D. Donaldson. 2 vols., EETS OS 39, 56, 1869, 1874.
Jerome. *Commentaire sur Jonas*. Edited and translated by Yves-Marie Duval, Éditions du Cerf, 1985.
Langland, William. *The Vision of Piers Plowman: A Complete Edition of the B Text*. Edited by A.V.C. Schmidt, Dent, 1984.
Marbod of Rennes. *Naufragium Jonae Prophetae. Patrologia Latina*, vol. 171, 1675–78.
The Meaning of the Glorious Quran. Edited and translated by Mohammed Marmaduke Pickthall. Government of India Central Press, 1938. www.sacred-texts.com/isl/pick/index.htm#contents.
Michel, Dan. *Ayenbite of Inwit or Remorse of Conscience*. Edited by Richard Morris, EETS OS 23, 1866.
Middle English Dictionary. Edited by Hans Kurath et al. U of Michigan P, 1952–, https://quod.lib.umich.edu/m/middle-english-dictionary/dictionary.
A Middle English Metrical Paraphrase of the Old Testament. Edited by Herbert Kalén and Urban Ohlander. Vol. 3, Elanders Boktr, 1923–72.
The Middle English Physiologus. Edited by Hanneke Wirtjes. EETS OS 299, 1999.
Patrologia Latina. Edited by Jacques-Paul Migne. 221 vols., 1844–65. https://www.proquest.com/patrologialatina.
Speculum Sacerdotale. Edited by Edward H. Weatherly. EETS OS, 200, 1936.

Criticism on *Patience*

Anderson, J.J., et al., *Language and Imagination in the Gawain Poems*. U of Manchester P, 2020.
Andrew, Malcolm. "Jonah and Christ in *Patience*." *Modern Philology*, vol. 70, no. 3, 1973, pp. 230–33.
———. "'Rome-runners' and *Patience*, line 52." *Archiv für das Studium der Neueren Sprachen und Literaturen*, vol. 219, 1982, pp. 116–18.
———. "Theories of Authorship." Brewer and Gibson, pp. 23–33.
Benson, C.D. "The Impatient Reader of *Patience*." Blanch et al., pp. 147–62.
Bernau, Anke. "Translating Form with *Patience*." *The Medieval Literary: Beyond Form*, edited by Robert J. Meyer-Lee and Catherine Sanok, Brewer, 2018, pp. 161–83.

Blanch, R., et al. *Text and Matter: New Critical Perspectives of the Pearl-Poet*. Whitson, 1991.

Bowers, John M. *An Introduction to the Gawain Poet*. U of Florida P, 2013.

Brewer, Derek, and Jonathan Gibson. *A Companion to the Gawain-Poet*. D.S. Brewer, 1999.

Craun, Edwin D. *Lies, Slander, and Obscenity in Medieval English Literature: Pastoral Rhetoric and the Deviant Speaker*. U of Cambridge P, 1997.

Davenport, W.A. *The Art of the Gawain-Poet*. Athlone, 1978.

Diekstra, F. "Jonah and *Patience*: The Psychology of a Prophet." *English Studies*, vol. 55, no. 3, 1974, pp. 205–17.

Friedman, J.B. "Figural Typology in the Middle English *Patience*." *The Alliterative Tradition in the Fourteenth Century*, edited by B.S. Levy and P.E. Szarmach, Kent State UP, 1981, pp. 99–129.

Gustafson, Kevin. "Speech and Translation in *Patience*." *Neophilologus*, vol. 106, no. 4, 2022, pp. 495–511.

Hatt, Cecilia A. *God and the Gawain-poet: Theology and Genre in Pearl, Cleanness, Patience and Sir Gawain and the Green Knight*. D.S. Brewer, 2015.

Jacobs, Nicolas, "Alliterative Storms: A Topos in Middle English." *Speculum*, vol. 47, no. 4, 1972, pp. 695–719.

Kirk, E. "'Who suffreth more than God?' Narrative Redefinition of Patience in *Patience* and *Piers Plowman*." *The Triumph of Patience*, edited by Gerald J. Schiffhorst, U of Florida P, 1978, pp. 88–105.

Lawton, David A. "The Diversity of Middle English Alliterative Poetry." *Leeds Studies in English*, vol. 20, 1989, pp. 143–72.

Neuhauser, R., "Scriptural and Devotional Sources." Brewer and Gibson, pp. 257–75.

Putter, Ad. *An Introduction to the Gawain-Poet*. Longman, 1996.

Putter, Ad, and Myra Stokes. "The *Linguistic Atlas* and the Dialect of the *Gawain* Poems." *Journal of English and Germanic Philology*, vol. 106, no. 4, 2007, pp. 469–91.

Schleusner, J. "History and Action in *Patience*." *PMLA*, vol. 86, no. 5, 1971, pp. 959–65.

Spearing, A.C. *The Gawain Poet: A Critical Study*. Cambridge UP, 1970.

Staley, Lynn. *The Voice of the Gawain-Poet*. U of Wisconsin P, 1984.

Stanbury, Sarah. *Seeing the Gawain-Poet: Description and the Act of Perception*. U of Pennsylvania P, 2017.

Stock, L.K. "The 'poynt' of *Patience*." Blanch et al., pp. 163–75.

Stokes, Myra. "'Suffering' in *Patience*." *Chaucer Review*, vol. 18, 1984, pp. 354–63.

Turville-Petre, Thorlac. *Description and Narrative in Middle English Alliterative Poetry*. U of Exeter P, 2018.

General and Contextual Reading

Armitage, Simon. *A Vertical Art: On Poetry*. Princeton UP, 2021.
Bennett, Michael J. *Community, Class and Careerism: Cheshire and Lancashire Society in the Age of "Sir Gawain and the Green Knight."* Cambridge UP, 1993.
Bowers, John M. *The Politics of* Pearl: *Court Poetry in the Age of Richard II*. D.S. Brewer, 2001.
Hudson, Anne. *The Premature Reformation: Wycliffite Texts and Lollard History*. Clarendon, 1988.
Putter, Ad, et al. *Studies in the Metre of Alliterative Verse*. Oxford UP, 2007.
Rice, Nicole. *Lay Piety and Religious Discipline in Middle English Literature*. Cambridge UP, 2008.
Somerset, Fiona. *Clerical Discourse and Lay Audience in Late Medieval England*. Cambridge UP, 1998.
Varnam, Laura. *The Church as Sacred Space in Middle English Literature and Culture*. Manchester UP, 2011.
Wallace, David. "*Cleanness* and the Terms of Terror." Blanch et al., pp. 93–100.
Watson, Nicholas, "The *Gawain* Poet as a Vernacular Theologian." Brewer and Gibson, pp. 93–313.

Image Credits

Pages 113–15: From the British Library/Bridgeman Images.

Page 116: Image courtesy of the Metropolitan Museum of Art.

Page 117: geogphotos/Alamy Stock Photo.

About the Publisher

The word "broadview" expresses a good deal of the philosophy behind our company. Our focus is very much on the humanities and social sciences—especially literature, writing, and philosophy—but within these fields we are open to a broad range of academic approaches and political viewpoints. We strive in particular to produce high-quality, pedagogically useful books for higher education classrooms—anthologies, editions, sourcebooks, surveys of particular academic fields and sub-fields, and also course texts for subjects such as composition, business communication, and critical thinking. We welcome the perspectives of authors from marginalized and underrepresented groups, and we have a strong commitment to the environment. We publish English-language works and translations from many parts of the world, and our books are available world-wide; we also publish a select list of titles with a specifically Canadian emphasis.

broadview press

The interior of this book is printed on 100% recycled paper.